THE AUDIENCE MAKES THE SHOW

& other insights, prose, and plays

by

Eric "Wally" Wallach

Copyright © 2024 Eric "Wally" Wallach

All rights reserved.

"The Presence of the Audience" was originally published in The Bridge Journal. "It's Not a Safe Space but It's Where We Live" and "Interview or Who's Afraid of Mr. Albee?" were both originally published in The Brooklyn Rail.

Front cover features *The Breasts of Tiresias* in Paris, 2010, photo credit to Alejandro Guerro who also took the author's photo. All other photos are by Wally unless otherwise noted. The back cover is of the Globe Theatre in London, 2023.

No part of this book may be used or reproduced, distributed, or transmitted in any form or by any means, including photocopying, recording, or other electronic or mechanical methods, without the proper written permission of the publisher, except in the case of brief quotations apart, embodied in critical reviews and certain other non-commercial uses permitted by copyright law. Use of this publication is permitted solely for personal use and must include full attribution of the material's source.

Paperback ISBN: 9798335648813

Imprint: Independently published

Peace!

(l to r) Josh Diamond, Ruby Sunrise, Captain Wally, and Lou on the maiden voyage of FLIGHT18.

DEDICATION

Dedicated to Ruby Sunrise and Lou Moonlight with my infinite love. This book is the best I have to offer you. Enjoy.

GRATITUDE

An ocean of gratitude to my family and friends especially my partner and love, Belinda Blum. An abundance of thanks to Barbara Spindel who has edited much of this. Thanks also to Lyn Haber for the editing support and more. Thanks also to my mom Mary and brother Benjamin. Thanks also to the big voices that are quoted here, namely playwright Edward Albee, director Robert Wilson, poet Guillaume Apollinaire, theatre artist Julian Beck of the Living Theatre, composer/writer/rock star Stew, and my father-in-love Elliot Blum.

Finally, thanks to you for reading.

TABLE OF CONTENTS

Safety Instructions	5
A Love Affair with Theatre	6
Wally's Theatric Formula	8
Theatre Senses	10
"I am from"	12
Quotes and "Questions" by Julian Beck	13
"The Presence of the Audience"	18
"Listening to Robert Wilson"	25
"Twilight on the Lower East Side"	32
"It's Not a Safe Space but It's Where We Live"	44
"Riding Until We Get There"	47
Backgammon Rules	49
Advice for Daddy-Doulas	55
How to Fly in Manhattan: a biker's guide	57
"Get Out of Egypt" and color songs	62
Moses in Five Acts	66
The Tale of the Thanksgiving Ladybug	70
The Breasts of Tiresias: A Surrealist Musical	77
Interview or Who's Afraid of Mr. Albee?	122

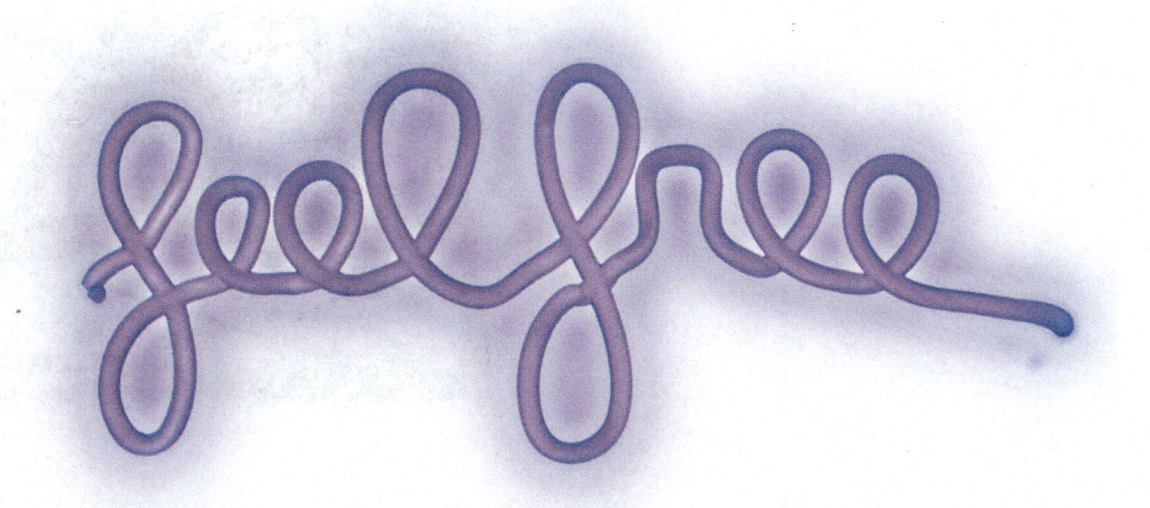

SAFETY INSTRUCTIONS
from FLIGHT18

Please keep eyes, ears, body, heart, and mind open at all times.

In case of an emergency, panic for five seconds before calmly breathing and accepting the moment as it is then hold the person or persons nearest to you.

We are all in this together.

Know that when you voyage into outer space you are taking your life into your own hands. Please take this opportunity to introduce yourself to your neighbors.

A LOVE AFFAIR WITH THEATRE

Honestly, my affair with the theatre is not a casual one. It was fascination at first sight at the Great American Melodrama and Vaudeville in California, 1978.

Eating popcorn, singing songs, and booing the villain, it was more fun than anything I could imagine and cathartic too. Here is a private place, where one could be alone while with others, in a room, playing out our fear and joy together, collectively rooting for a happy ending. When I met the actors after the show and started my autograph collection the whole world fell into place. At six years old, I knew what I could do with my life.

When I was eight years old, I played a gravedigger for the Haunted House, at my neighborhood recreation center, scaring people who walked past me. Jump scares. I was cast as Hugo F. Peabody in *Bye Bye Birdie* in seventh grade, performed in the school's "Multi-Purpose Room". When I was fourteen, I began a holy communion with Shakespeare, weeping as I read *Romeo and Juliet*, learning what love is.

That same year, my mom took me to see a cavernous art show, like a two-ring circus, by Jonathan Borofsky and Red Grooms at the Temporary Contemporary Museum in Los Angeles. It was both scary and mind-blowing, with realistic-looking children falling from the ceiling and on the walls were scrawled in charcoal dream anecdotes. I walked through a larger-than-life brightly colored subway car that rocked as you went through it, past disinterested characters.

This is me fluctuating between a deep appreciation for theatre and the mystery of spectacular art. I was anointed a "Child o' the Theatre" as a freshman in High School. By Summer 1989, I gave up my virginity at Cal Arts while I attended the California State Summer School of the Arts where I also began collaborating with artists and poets of all kinds, each who stirred my imagination and inspired.

June of 1990, I produced and directed my first full-length show, *The Curate Shakespeare As You Like It* by Don Nigro. In an article in the *Los Angeles Times*, I was quoted saying, "I will never, never produce again." The joke was on me. Between there and here, I have produced, written, and directed many, many shows, plays, dances, musicals, public art performances, and art installations. Almost all of them have included the audience as an integral part of the happening. This has always been my obsession, to connect, to feel less alone, to share in the wonderment of this existence.

In 1990, I saw *Hip-Hop Waltz of Eurydice* created by Reza Abdoh at Los Angeles Theatre Center and it ripped the theatre apart, screaming for freedom. From then on, my only ambition was to create a theatre that was free. Broadway was taken off the map. Later in the summer, in London, I saw *The Wild Duck* and learned from the production that lies can kill. I was sick for a week after it (the guilt of many lies and broken hearts). From then on, I could only stomach a theatre that is honest and real.

When I arrived to New York City I began experiencing theatre from every vantage point possible as Stage Crew, Stage Manager, Lighting Designer, Actor, Playwright, Director, Producer, Teacher, Acting Coach, and telemarketer! My favorite perspective will always be as an audience member. I need a consistent flow of new provocations to keep the affair hot.

I steer clear of theatre that is created in a vacuum or worse, on a golf course. I want something to challenge me. I want theatre to transform me. I want the play to be an instrument of public discourse that inspires radical change.

Through my long relationship with theatre, I've learned this: the audience makes the show. We get what we put in. Finally, we will better know our selves by what we remember, by the stories we tell and by the visions we have. We also know ourselves by our ACTION! So, let's get into it.

7

WALLY'S THEATRIC FORMULA
W.T.F.?!

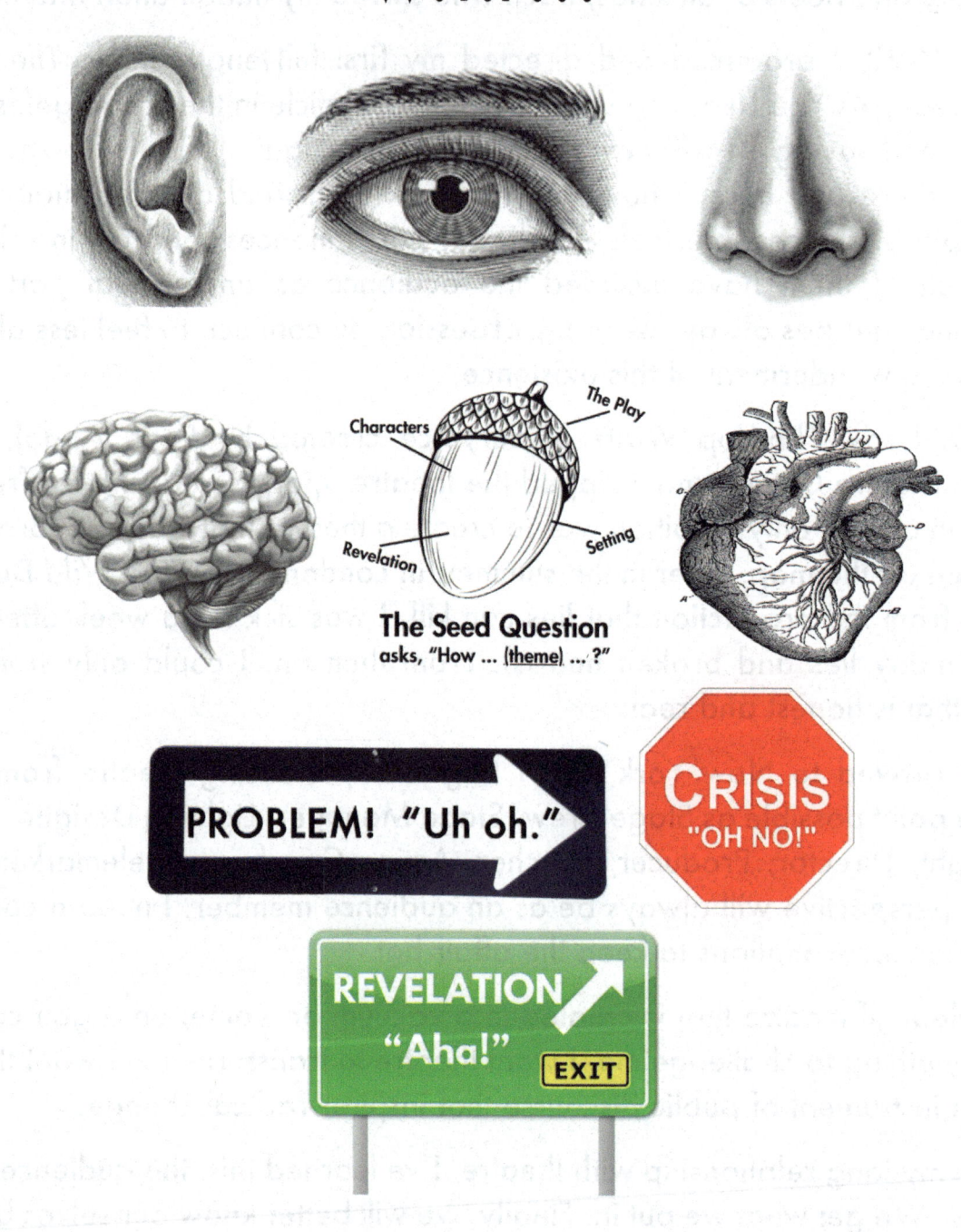

Characters — The Play — Setting — Revelation

The Seed Question
asks, "How ... (theme) ...?"

PROBLEM! "Uh oh."

CRISIS "OH NO!"

REVELATION "Aha!" EXIT

WHAT do you see hear, see, feel, and think about life and the world around you?

We approach theatre-making as a place where everyone has a role to play from playwright to member of the audience. At the center of it all are the essential questions, WHO AM I? WHO ARE WE?

In life and theatre there exists a circular journey of questioning. First, we use the magnifying glasses to determine the WHATs that we're observing. Next, we wonder through the telescope asking, HOW __? Before we move from that spot we dig, researching where we are with our WHY shovel. When the time comes, we get out the test tube and begin imagining, WHAT IF? Observe what you create and let it grow on its own.

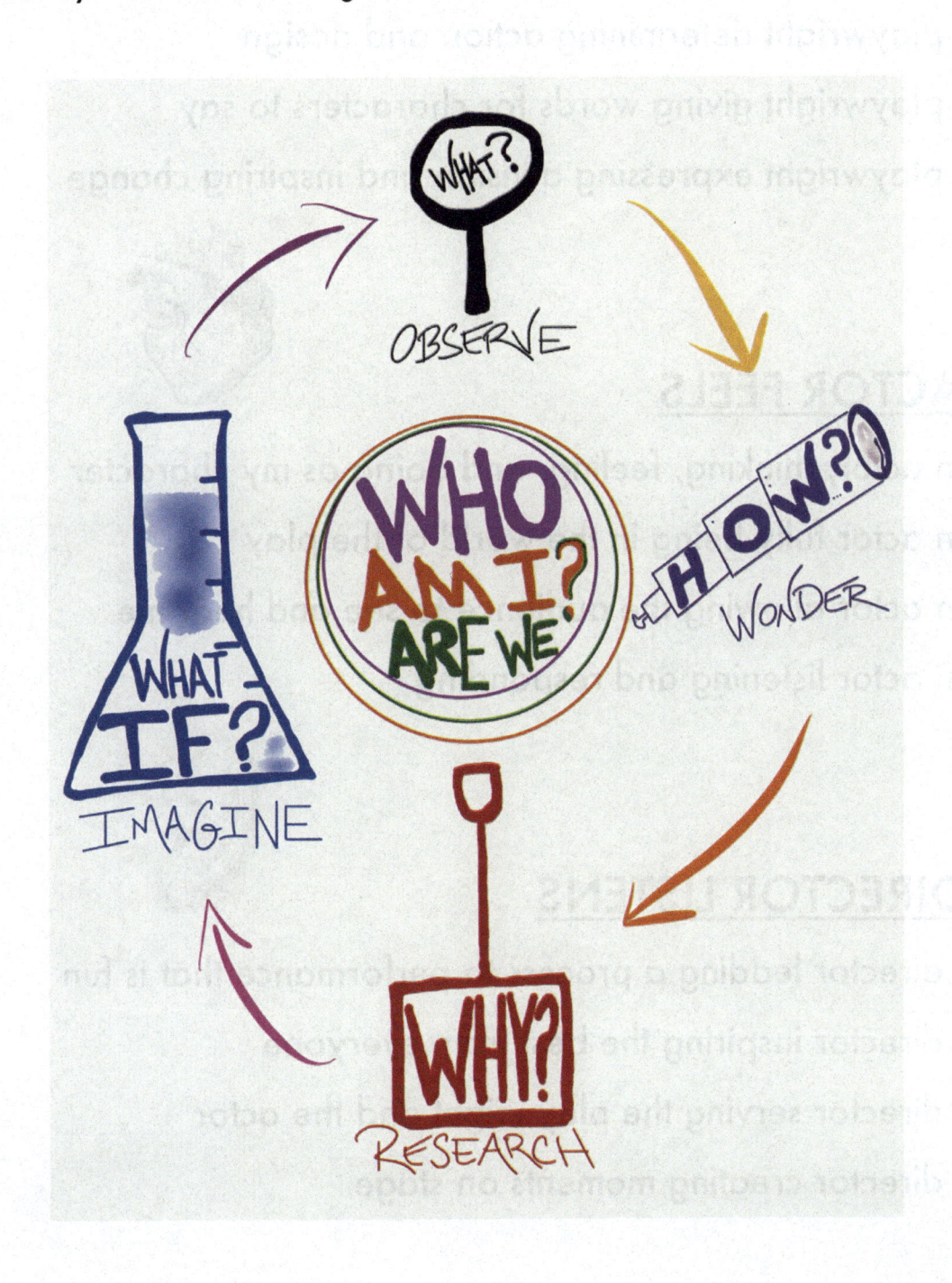

THEATRE SENSES

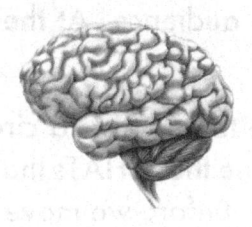

THE PLAYWRIGHT THINKS

I am a storyteller showing and solving problems

I am a playwright determining action and design

I am a playwright giving words for characters to say

I am a playwright expressing a vision and inspiring change

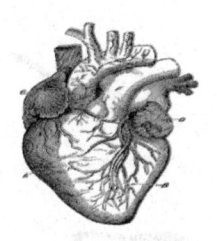

THE ACTOR FEELS

I am an actor, thinking, feeling, and doing as my character

I am an actor fully being in the world of the play

I am an actor allowing the audience to see and hear me

I am an actor listening and responding

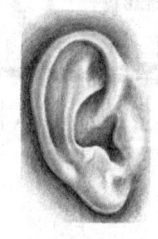

THE DIRECTOR LISTENS

I am a director leading a process to performance that is fun

I am a director inspiring the best from everyone

I am a director serving the playwright and the actor

I am a director creating moments on stage

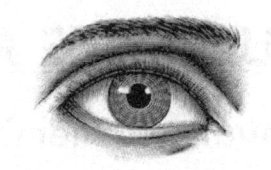

THE DESIGNER SEES

I am a set designer creating the look of the physical show

I am a costume designer collaborating with actors and team

I am a light designer composing the movement and color of light

I am a sound designer choosing music and sound

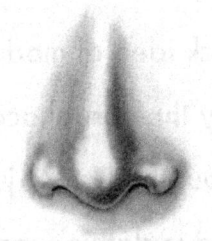

THE STAGE MANAGER KNOWS

I am a stage manager sticking my nose in everything, sensing what's going on, remembering the details, and ensuring safe, careful play.

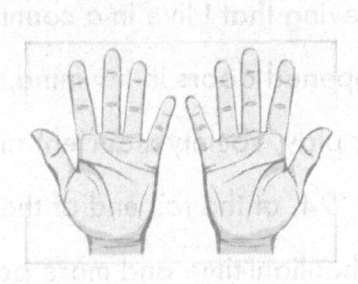

THE CREW IS HANDS ON

I am on hair and make-up drawing character

I am a costume crewmember checking every stitch

I am a prop crewmember giving actors what they need

I am a stage crewmember changing the set

I am a board operator running the lights and sound

THE AUDIENCE MEMBER QUESTIONS

I am an audience member seeking stories, observing details, listening, and paying attention, and questioning what I see.

I am from

By Wally

I am from a sick idea of modernity, the Valley, just off the Ronald Reagan freeway

Surrounded by the casual acceptance of mediocrity like a thick smog

Found out about the U.S.A. just before graduating high school in Humanities

I had protested malathion-spraying, bomb testing and South African apartheid

Marched for action to help those living with HIV/AIDS

I became politically active as soon as I knew I could

I like believing that I live in a country that can fix its mistakes

Theatre opened doors in my mind, from Beckett to Baraka, from Fugard to Albee

Play after play, society's ancient and present rot becoming clear

N.Y.C. in '94, at the tail end of the very end of the Big Juicy Apple

Before Ghouliani-time and more police, more police state, more need to fight the Man

Enter the Living Theatre, Open Theatre, theatre happening with, by and for the People

The Battle in Seattle, whose streets? pushing back on the corporatocracy

I am from the books I've read and the Village souls that talked with me

I am from the struggle since my great-grandparents landed here a hundred years ago

I am from the radical that's left and left of the Radical Left

As Judith Malina coined, I am for the Beautiful Non-Violent Anarchist Revolution

I am from a long line of voyagers into the Unknown

BEING AN OBSERVER QUOTES

"In a grand sense, I do what you
do and you do what I do.
Thus it is economical for each
one of us to be original. We get
more done by not doing what
someone else is doing. This
way we can speed up history –
the one we're making. No need
for competition, even with
oneself. After all, we're all
the same species and we live on the
same planet. And I am not who I was.

We were artisans; now we're
the observers of miracle. All you
have to do is go straight on,
leaving the path at any moment,
and to the right or the left,
coming back or never, coming
in, of course, out of the rain."

– John Cage, *Where are we going? And what are we doing?*

"You must enter the theatre through the world. All niceness must then be exploded. To make something useful. To provide the useful event that can help us. A theatre not for the people, but at one with people. The theatre of change. Of emergency. Of feeling. When we feel, we will feel the emergency: when we feel the emergency, we will act, when we act, we will change the world. Art is not a profession but a path toward truth both for maker and spectator."
- Julian Beck, *The Life of the Theatre*

QUESTIONS 1963/1968

by Julian Beck

The Life of the Theatre - the relation of the artist to the struggle of the people
published 1972, City Lights Books - edited for performance by Wally

what is the difference between questions and answers

is hamlet's questioning his glory or his tragedy

why do you go to the theatre

is it important to go to the theatre

is it important to read

do people who go to the theatre differ from people who don't go to the theatre

what happens to you if you go to the theatre

when you leave the theatre have you changed that is of course you are changed by each moment of experience so three hours later you are naturally different but i mean have you changed actively

do you want to change actively

are you content

is it good to change

is anything sufficient unchanged

what am i talking about

do you go to the theatre for answers

do you have any questions

what is happening to us

what happens in the theatre

do you go to the theatre to find out about life

is it easier to observe life in the theatre or in the street

have you experienced joy in the theatre

have you experienced joy in the street

what do you enjoy

are you content i ask again

are you content with anything

do you have satisfactory sex

i mean do you like it when you have it

do you have enough of it

do you know how to love

do you love

are you loved

do you know how to hate

and do you

why do i prefer a disturbing theatre to a pleasing one tho i like to please

do you know that i have reached into my entrails and strewn them about the stage in the form of questions

do you know that i do not know what else to do

do you know that i need you that i am dying and will die without you

what is useful

what is a good question

what is a way to find answers

what will knock down the prison walls

what is the way

what is the relationship between the actor and the spectator

what is speech

what is important inquiry

do we have time enough to ask all the questions

which ones do you want to ask

will you ask them now

what do we need

how can we get it

how can we touch one another

how can we make it happen

how can we make a theatre which makes love love now

how can we make a theatre which is worthy of the life of its spectators

how can we make a theatre when we do not know any answers but only have vague hints about how to ask questions

how do we feed all the people

how do we stop all the wars

how do we open the doors of all the jails

how do we disintegrate the violence

how do we obliterate racism

how do we get rid of money (capitalism)

how do we undo early death

how do we end militarism

how do we put an end to authoritarian systems

how do we end the class system thing

how do we find the answers to these questions

how do we do it now

i end with questions because i have no answers

but what i want is answers

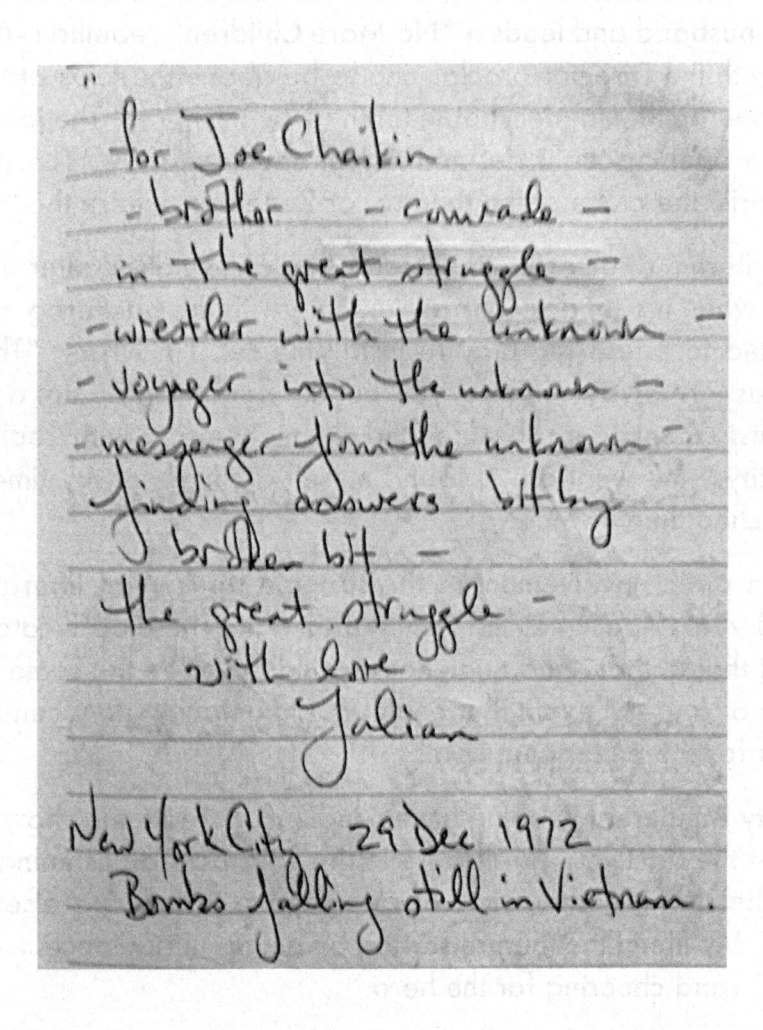

> for Joe Chaikin
> – brother – comrade –
> in the great struggle –
> – wrestler with the unknown –
> – voyager into the unknown –
> – messenger from the unknown –
> finding answers bit by
> bit –
> the great struggle –
> with love
> Julian
>
> New York City 29 Dec 1972
> Bombs falling still in Vietnam.

My theatre father is director Joe Chaikin. I found this inscription in Joe's copy of Julian Beck's *The Life of the Theatre*. I wrote it in my journal.

THE PRESENCE OF THE AUDIENCE:

Political Theatre in Today's World

for Judith Malina and the Beautiful Anarchist Nonviolent Revolution

"Total theatre needs universality of spirit. A theatre for vast audiences ... revealing the reverence of man for man." – Erwin Piscator

In 1917 Paris, poet Guillaume Apollinaire's *The Breasts of Tiresias* deliberately pried open the theatre and gave birth to the first revolutionary transsexual. Therese, now Tiresias, sacrifices her breasts in an act of self-mutilation with balloons and scissors, changes clothes with her husband and leads a "No More Children" rebellion. Apollinaire's Prologue defiantly begins with the Director proclaiming to be above the laws of the government and ends with, "O people, be the unquenchable torch of the new fire." The joining of forces with the audience led to an opening night riot midway through the show. The audience split over where they were: Paris, the place of the theatre, or Zanzibar, where the "surrealist drama" was set.

In 1920 Berlin, director Erwin Piscator had a revelation after a spontaneous moment stopped his play when his set designer arrived late with the backdrop over his shoulder. The audience demanded to pause the play to install the set. He wrote, "The curtain separating life from stage was torn away. Theatre, yes, but a different kind – not a stage, but a platform – theatre as an instrument to probe life and come to grips with reality – not an audience, but a community." He went on, "I found myself a citizen of my time. The interplay of art and life had reached unity for me."

Theatre's direct involvement in the struggle for human liberation reached a new level one hundred years ago, after the First World War. The global catastrophe of loss and shock was so great that authors and audiences would never be the same again. A pursuit began for the creation of a useful event that could assist humanity. Between the Wars humans tried coming together for the betterment of all.

Creativity is inherent in being alive. Audiences create the show just as much as the performers do when they actively participate in the spectacle by listening and observing. The audience makes the show by their natural response so if they are elsewhere the theatrical endeavor falls flat. My life in the theatre started by being an audience member at a melodrama, booing the villain and cheering for the hero.

I moved to New York City in 1994, which was the tail end of the end of what once was the Big Apple. Now it's the "Big Cupcake", as performing artist Penny Arcade says. In the mid-

90s, before gentrification took over, real human interaction was still possible all the time. A chance meeting could change your life.

Three days after 1998 rolled in I got calls from two theatre greats, Penny Arcade and Joseph Chaikin. For five years I rode out the disappearance of Bohemia between them both, on the Lower East Side and the West Village, respectively. Their primary concern has always been their community and the exploration of existence through performance. The west and east sides of lower Manhattan have had differing approaches to the stage, experimental and erudite on the west side and rock'n'roll glitter on the east.

I received the secret history of New York's political theatre from two strains of thought: from Jack Smith to John Vaccaro to Penny Arcade to me and from Piscator to Julian Beck and Judith Malina to Joe Chaikin to me. A responsibility came attached to these histories to continue the struggle, carry the torch, thoughtfully and with verve.

I've tried many events on and off the stage. The last eighteen years have demanded action from us, and yet large demonstrations have been mostly ineffective; the wars haven't stopped, corruption continues unabated.

After months of guilt and broken spirit following the reelection of George W. Bush, I went to Costa Rica for my 33rd birthday and enjoyed the pure, military-free life there. At Jesus Christ's age when he was crucified, I had a vision of the Prince of Peace in the USA. When I returned to the city, I wrote a short play and set it a few blocks from my East Village home.

American Terrorist a random act

A 33-year-old Jew, with black curly hair and beard, wearing a blue sarong diaper and upside-down American flag cape ascends a New York City signpost. Across his lower body is written "TRY PEACE" in red. His arms are held to either side by a long narrow piece of wood.

He stands up there in silence for at least five hours and no longer than twelve days or for as long as New York City can tolerate free speech.

Over 18,000 civilians have died during our two-year-old Iraq War. This is dedicated to all those humans who have been senselessly murdered.

Tuesday, April 25, 2005 Astor Place 3pm

I had four months to prepare the action, which was just enough time to grow a beard, scope the scene, and refine the costume into an American flag sarong, a crown of ripped money, and the words "ALL-AMERICAN" written in stage blood across my chest. The title changed to *Radical Jew, 33*.

A week prior to the action I called the editor of my neighborhood newspaper *The Villager*, Lincoln Anderson, and told him the plan. When he asked me why I was doing it, I answered simply, "I just can't stand the war."

On the night before the action, I installed a sign just above where I was to perch myself that read: WAR? I also doctored, with white gaffers tape, the two ONE-WAY signs on the street pole to read: NO WAY and NO WAR. As it was the second night of Passover, I drank a little wine and ate some matzo before sleep. In the morning I was quiet and resolute. Around noon I walked barefoot out my door. I carried my white birch branch, with glimmering red fabric tied in loops at either end, to my crucifixion in Astor Place.

I pulled myself up and onto the signpost and stood on the arm that held a walk sign. I positioned the stick behind my neck, put my hands through the loops and that was that. What will the people do when I'm up there? What will they do when the cops come? I had no idea what was going to happen. What happened was better than any play I could have written. The real world met my fantasy and performed well.

Some people passed by while others stopped and stayed with me for a while. Some jeered and mocked me. Others were scared. And the flow of traffic never stopped.

The weather had gone from sunny to gray and breezy. I shivered and shed tears. Though I felt safe as a performer, I was overwhelmed with sadness at times. From time to time, I was buoyed by the support of strangers. Someone raised a two-fingered peace sign to me; another person spoke out.

After an hour and a half, things began to shift again when the seventh police vehicle I saw came to a stop below. Through the car megaphone I was asked to get down. The officers asked a few times before more cars arrived. A crowd began forming as a news crew happened upon the scene. Eventually an Emergency Vehicle parked alongside the back of the pole.

The officers standing on the Emergency Vehicle roof looked like three Romans as they carefully cut one of the red loops of fabric. I remained passive and let my hand fall. The branch slipped away, and I was gracefully carried off the cross. Atop the vehicle they strapped me to a board and prepared to lower me through a hatch in the roof.

When they lifted me upright to lower me down, I took a moment to look out at everyone. The people had the chance to be the show in that moment. I saw no riots, no struggle, just a smattering of applause.

Imagine what would've happened if it had been 2015. #goingviral As Astor Place has been recently redesigned, I have committed myself to a resurrection of political action of some sort on this bit of land that was once a crossroad for native American footpaths.

New York City has turned the once fecund ground of cross-fertilized art into a comparatively barren arts cityscape even though theatre is, more than ever, essential to our collective well-being. Here now is a time and place when we can feel the energy of real people en masse and they're not cheering at a ballgame, they're listening. Theatre can be a tool for social reform when artists cross-pollinate and conspire.

Unfortunately, in our fair city, even radical theatre cannot afford a conspiracy of artists and yet it is now one of the only places that a group of people can congregate without risking arrest. Today only the wealthy can afford the real estate or the ticket prices. Discontent and moral outrage mixed with the complacency of consumer culture has given birth to a cry for social transformation in the most popular of Broadway musicals on the ol' Great White Way. Look no further than the wildly successful productions of *Matilda*, *Wicked*, *Kinky Boots*, and now *Hamilton* to realize that if the United States could exist in today's Broadway musical, the second American Revolution would be close at hand.

By the end of *Kinky Boots*, the working-class workers and trans-performers are uniting in order to empower each other. The big moment in both *Wicked* and *Matilda* arrives when it's revealed that those in power are utilizing a massive surveillance apparatus to keep the people in check–flying monkeys in one, red lasers in the other.

Matilda and her classmates get the audience clapping over their heads singing, "We are revolting children living in revolting times … we'll be revolting children, 'til our revolting's done – it's 2-L-8-4-U. We are revolting!" Audiences nod with recognition and satisfaction that they are witnessing real, safe, political theatre. Everybody wants to live in a world rid of tyranny! It makes for good theatre. Ka-ching!

Hamilton's raps are honest and straightforward yet the "buttons" that follow every other song are as unnecessary as the buttons on a Revolutionary coat. The "button" is that extra bump up of music and light that lets an audience know that the song is over, and the actors will pause for applause. It feels like a counterbalance to the use of hip-hop, establishing the show as part of the musical theatre canon, not as a call to arms.

As with seeing art in museums, politics are deadened in the theatre because of its inherent impotence. There's no consequence or immediacy. There's a bribe that says, "I'll pay you good money if you make me feel I'm seeing something significant, but don't go so far as to offend me." We get musicals where there could be movements.

Gratefully, the struggle continues in the 21st century with agents provocateurs such as The Yes Men who have shown how theatre can happen anywhere and at any time and the right actions can effect change. Such was the time when Andy Bichlbaum impersonated a Dow Chemical representative named Jude Finisterra and announced on BBC World TV that Dow would compensate the victims of Dow's disaster in Bhopal and would clean up the mess. Dow's stock fell 4.24 percent in 23 minutes, wiping two billion dollars off its market value. Yes, theatre can.

Perhaps if political theatre wants to catch the kings and their subjects then it may have to continue to infiltrate the world. Creative direct public action has the potential to pierce our consumer culture in pursuit of a world community. Now is the time to see what we can do with the balance of life and our art.

Since 2002, when I premiered my show FLIGHT18, I have sought ways of engaging today's community aboard my Spaceship Kaleidoscope, where audience members, recast as passengers, meet, and play as they cruise round-trip through our solar system. Now, as governments and politicians continue their downward spiral, FLIGHT18 will turn public space into outer space.

My third incarnation of FLIGHT18 is called Kaleidoscoping, and it involves an easy-to-follow inclusive choreographic game built on the exchange of dance moves. We mirror and multiply what is there. On June 7, 2016 we launched from Governor's Island, Grand Central Station, and finally, Times Square.

As war is brought to our streets, clubs, stadiums, and halls, so must our action. For every bomb that is dropped, droned, shot, or thrown, let there be a large-scale act of love or beauty in public. The sight of people dancing freely in public is political theatre enough. No banners or pronouncements or calls for peace and justice. Just dance and the revolution will follow.

The ensemble of FLIGHT18 posing in Times Square, 2014.

Wally starring as *Radical Jew, 33* in Astor Place, April 2005.
The public art performance protesting the wars lasted two hours.

The Passion of Astor Pl.

As a protest against the U.S. war in Iraq, Eric Wallach of the East Village staged his own crucifixion at the Astor Pl. traffic triangle at Lafayette St., from where the Cube sculpture was recently removed for repairs. To crucify himself at the East Village crossroads, Wallach climbed on top of a crossing-signal sign, tied his wrists to a crossbeam and perched there about two hours. Passersby snapped photos of him with their cellphone cameras, but when onlookers began to crowd the island, police moved them off. The expression on Wallach's face was of ecstasy, though at times he appeared to be actually crying. Modern-day centurions of a sort, three police officers took him down from his "cross," handcuffed him, put him on a backboard and loaded him into a police vehicle. Wallach, who also goes by the moniker Radical Jew 33, is a freelance theater artist and self-described "provocateur." "I just can't stand the war," he told The Villager.

JESUS GETS OFF: Speaking of mock crucifixions, Eric Wallach tells us that for doing his Jesus-on-the-cross performance on an Astor Pl. street light to protest the Iraq war, he was given an adjournment in contemplation of dismissal with three days of community service in Tompkins Square Park. Provided he stays out of trouble — and doesn't crucify himself again — the incident will be cleared from his record after six months.

Another view of 'crucifixion'

Eric Wallach, 33, was removed on a body board after he staged a mock crucifixion on Tuesday at Astor Pl. in protest of the Iraq war. Wallach has worked with well-known performance artist Penny Arcade.

Photos by Bob Arihood.

LISTENING TO ROBERT WILSON

"Our ears are in excellent condition."

- John Cage

Robert Wilson's life is a never-ending line of artistic pursuits. He has discovered new territories in opera, theatre, music/theatre, and the visual arts. Tom Waits, William Burroughs, Philip Glass and David Byrne have all collaborated with him and he has staged the works of Bertolt Brecht, Richard Wagner, Gertrude Stein and Henrik Ibsen among many others. Wilson has even starred in his own *Hamlet, a monologue*.

The first time I heard of Robert Wilson was from a documentary about Wilson's groundbreaking five-hour opera *Einstein on the Beach*. In 1974, Wilson rented the Metropolitan Opera on a dark night to debut his collaboration with Mr. Glass which was made famous by the eighteen-minute scene that focused entirely on a bar of light moving from a horizontal position to a vertical position.

When Wilson was asked about what he was trying to achieve with *Einstein*, he answered with a kind of riddle. "When someone puts a candelabra on top of a grand piano, that's one thing; but when someone puts a candelabra on a boulder, that's something else. And I got to thinking, maybe people could see that candelabra a bit easier if it were on top of a boulder instead."

After much letter-writing a brief assignment came up for me to assist Wilson during the development of a new piece with the Martha Graham Dance Company. This was back in the mid-'90s when Wilson's assistants had to carry a duffle bag that contained three huge address books. In rehearsals, Wilson would demand absolute stillness and silence before he'd quietly command, "Play the music." Following the impulse of Lou Harrison's Balinese music, he would then dance freely through the space while assistants and dancers took note.

During that short time with Wilson, he inadvertently taught me that the space between things opened doorways to creative sustenance and that patience reveals mystery. For Wilson, looking and seeing is an active sport; the only rule is to listen.

Over the four decades that he has been working those who work with or for Wilson affectionately call him Bob. While his manner is calculated, Bob himself is warm, charming, and generous. I got permission to interview him on the premise that I was writing for an academic theatre periodical. When Bob asked me what the interview was to be about, I said, "Your theatre." He responded earnestly, "I think you should write about Watermill."

The Watermill Center is Bob's most personal and ambitious project. Firmly rooted after fifteen years at his hub in Water Mill, Long Island, Bob reaches across the world with his vision of art and life. Watermill's six acres of grasses and trees dotted with ancient stones surrounds the three-story rectangular grey building that once was a 30,000 square-foot Western Union telecommunications research laboratory. Bob continues to meticulously transform Watermill's design realizing the full potential of each space.

I come upon the ground-floor offices as it has no fourth wall but rather looks out on an expansive square lawn. Bob happens to pass through before I announce myself to an assistant, standing six-foot three inches tall and looking elegant in a black t-shirt, blue jeans, and black sneakers. He asks me to wait in a top floor room where I can watch him walking outside through the landscape with his clipboard.

After a while, an assistant directs me to meet Bob for an impromptu tour through his international studies center for the arts and humanities with a small group of friends who happen to be paying a visit. Though Bob has a strict calendar it seems to be defied by the real world every day. His schedule is so tight, he's usually in more than one place simultaneously.

We congregate on the flat black stones that cover the floor of Watermill's tall rectangular center vestibule. It's a holy space where one has the feeling of being both outside and inside simultaneously. Two tall rectangular open entryways face east and west. The adjacent walls stand with two doors that lead to the north and south wings. Watermill's core is dense with mystery.

Bob begins quietly, "The Watermill Center is something unique in America. It's a Center in this community and then the community at large, a Center that I hope is here long after I'm no longer living." He goes on, "Architecture is about doors. Architecture is about buildings and trees. Architecture is about lines. Lastly, architecture is about time and space."

Walking to the eastern entryway Bob proclaims, "The Bible says, 'Behold! I sat before thee, an open door.' Here at Watermill the door is always open."

Pointing through the opening he adds, "Here you have an axis that goes from east to west. You can get out of a car, walk up here and go straight through to the end of the property." At the western opening he continues, "If you look out here, you will see a ring of stones in the trees which are three thousand years before Christ.

Bob says, "This building is the tallest vertical and it's in the center. The roof is floating, so rain, snow, light can all come in. If you stand on the roof of this building, you can only look up. It frames the sky.

"This floor has light under it washing the walls; it's floating. In the basement, the walls are illuminated as well. And in the center of the basement there's a well ... and that well goes to the center ... of the Earth. It is covered with a grid, and it has a sound, a drone." After a pause, Bob lets out a primordial drone that sounds like a toad on valium.

From the middle of the vestibule, he finishes, "Time for me is the vertical line that goes to the Heavens and goes to the center of the Earth. Space is a horizontal line. It is this cross of time and space and the tension between them that is the basic architecture of everything. It's how you stand on the stage. It's the drip of milk in a Vermeer painting. It's that stripe in a Barnett Newman painting."

"So, I can't really run through this," Bob says as he enters the space, "I have to take my time to walk." In a fast world, Bob takes it slow.

|

We leave our shoes at the door before entering the luminous Watermill interior space. The dustless floors are a polished dark brown wood. The abundance of windows fills the space with gradually shifting shapes of light. The white walls literally hover an inch above the floor. Each room is an open space that transforms easily from a gallery to living quarters or from a rehearsal hall to a performance space.

Just like Bob's theatrical productions, patient and deliberate, everything is perpetually in motion. Every now and again someone interrupts Bob about an errand or a project happening simultaneously someplace else to which he gives the order and continues on.

The Watermill International Summer Arts Program welcomes artists of all ages and disciplines to come to work with Bob. Each artist receives free room and board. Everyone participates in creative workshops and rehearsals with Bob while also taking classes from each other. Every free moment is dedicated to the hard labor of landscaping, moving trees, plants, and stones.

We enter a room that has one long white table. In the middle stands a large glass pitcher of chilled water with large slices of lemons and limes. "We have collaborative meetings here," Bob says as he sits down with a paper and pencil at hand.

As he talks, Bob draws a dot with a perfect circle around it, the astronomical symbol for the sun. "At the Center we have over thirty nations represented working in programs of theatre, architecture, music and arts-related projects. We are also developing satellite Watermills all around the world which will house projects that give the public a place for art and contemplation."

One project he's currently designing is a park just outside of London that for a hundred years was an ammunition site. Bob says, "The land was poisoned. So now we're replenishing the land, planting and letting nature take hold."

Getting up from the table, Bob moves to some architectural drawings for a renovation of a 50s movie house from Naples, Italy and two buildings in Stavanger, Norway, one which will be a meditation room with a forest of stones. "Watermill is an international center that's not in Paris or Rome," he says. Bob is creating extensions from the Ballroom in Marfa, Texas to an old fort in Toraja, Indonesia. He concludes, "Watermill is found in places that we normally wouldn't go to, so that to go there is something special."

We follow Bob out of the room and into his eclectic collection of art and artifacts from all over the world. The collection has over 9,000 pieces, and it grows at a rate of 300 pieces every year. Along with many museum-quality artworks there are hundreds of artifacts and textiles from various Indonesian cultures along with one of the largest privately held collections of chairs.

"On occasion you can take an object out and put it in a workstation," Bob says. "There are pieces here that date back to the Stone Age and they are not in glass boxes. The idea is that you don't have to go to a museum to see art. Here you can actually touch them, look at them. All the schools that I went to were like prisons... institutional green. At Watermill you live with an awareness of art all the time."

In one room an Isamu Noguchi stool sits next to a totem from northern Burma. In another part there's a flute from Mali beside 17th century Kabuki masks. A Man Ray photograph of Gertrude Stein hangs by a sheet of Merce Cunningham's notations and a portrait of John Cage. Chinese Neolithic pots commune with a white Eskimo stool made of walrus bone.

"This desk here is called 'Table for a Writer'. It was made for *The White Raven*," Bob says. The top of the table is filled with a few inches of water. Lotus flowers float where one expects a laptop, paper, or pen.

Inside a glass box is a pair of white high-heeled shoes with diamonds at the point of each stiletto. "These are Marlene Dietrich's favorite shoes. She had them on when she fell off stage during her last performance." Bob adds, "I went to visit Marlene before she died. She was in bed behind a screen. I asked her quietly, 'Marlene, who is the greatest?' After a moment she said, 'Tina Turner.'"

Bob then leads the group down into the temperature-controlled basement, the fallout shelter for his most precious relics. There's a photograph by Lee Miller of a dead Nazi with a clenched fist, a painting of Hitler behind him and out the window a Victory statue. Next to it is another photograph of a dead Nazi, this one in a ditch near Dachau.

In a long glass case there are Jerry Robbins' sneakers, George Balanchine's shoes, Rudolf Nureyev's ballet shoes from when he danced with Margaret Fontaine in *Sleeping Beauty*, with the blood stain still on the toe.

At last Bob lifts a translucent plate up to the light illuminating the fine white lines on the front and back. "This is very thin porcelain by the Danish ceramic artist Bodil Manz. You see the vertical and horizontal lines ... when light comes through you get the grid, the vertical and the horizontal."

+

Bob bids farewell to his friends and returns to the long table where he gives me the chance to ask a question. I ask about *The Fables of La Fontaine*, a play he had directed with the actors at the Comédie-Française in Paris.

He responds with subdued horror saying, "I was very surprised. I thought the acting would be formalized, not naturalistic or psychological but the Comédie-Française is just like Broadway. They both have a very exterior, head-orientated approach ... always about these I-DEE-AHS."

"In the 17th century theatre," Bob continues, "there were gestures ... a theatrical language that was learned. Everybody learned how to speak the text, how to stand on stage and how to walk.

"We have no clue today. Go to Julliard, go to Yale, Northwestern and look at these kids who are graduating. They come out of school and don't know how to stand or how to walk. They have no technique, it's all this ..." Bob starts to mime a smiling robot as his face grows pale. "What American actor can stand on the stage? I don't know one."

Bob has found wells of inspiration on different continents. When asked about his recent production of *I la Galigo* the blood comes back to his face. He says, "It was something different. This actor, he was eighteen years old, his father is the King of Toraja. He could just stand there ... noble and beautiful ... you felt something deep."

Is there a way to achieve this impact without being kin to royalty? Is there a method? "I think that one thinks with the body, the way an animal does", Bob says. "The way a dog walks to a bird, he's not listening with his ears, but the way the foot touches the floor, his body is listening."

A silence pervades the air. Bob puts forward a story, "I was in Berlin some years ago and I went to the zoo just before it was closing. There was a pack of grey wolves standing on rocks.

I walked up and stopped. And they were still. They didn't turn their heads to look at me but they were aware that I was standing there. We stood ... fifteen minutes. We were a pack together, one unit somehow ... the way we were listening to one another."

Bob adds with vigor, "Ezra Pound said, 'The fourth; the dimension of stillness. And the power over wild beasts.'"

When asked what the best way to prepare for the stage is he responds, "Empty one's head, get everything out. That's what I would do when I did Hamlet. Just try to think of nothing and let the piece come to me instead of me having to go to it. Actors are always trying to make a situation or singers are trying to make music." Bob shakes his head then says, "Receive music ... it's a gift. A good actor is someone who stays open; someone who performs for himself first and then allows the audience to come to them. So, it's not considered lightly to speak *at* someone like George Bush does ... you speak *with* a public.

"In the formal theatre there's a certain reserve. You are listening, the way the wolves were listening, to the audience. Ideally you become one muted entity, actors, musicians, audience. Listening is the most important thing in the theatre. The second most important thing is to have fun, that's why you make it. Nobody wants to see a depressing, heavy theatre."

Bob momentarily receives the Prince of Denmark. He is not acting but rather he's enjoying himself when he says, "How all occasions do inform against me, and spur my dull revenge! Examples gross as earth exhort me: witness this army of such mass and charge led by a delicate and tender prince, whose spirit with divine ambition puff'd makes mouths at the invisible event."

Bob says the word "mouths" as if he discovered it for the first time. "That's Hamlet. I learned that piece when I was twelve. I say it every day and every time I say it, I can think about it in a different way. If I start to impose *interpretations* or *ideas*, I lose the possibility of thinking about all the other things that it could be about. It's full of meaning.

"A good actor is not someone who is going to say what something is, but is going to say, 'What am I saying?' Then you have a dialogue. It's the space in back of you that's important," Bob says gesturing behind his neck. "The space back here, it sort of makes you noble. It's the space behind the words as well; it's the irony that's on the other side of the words that's important."

With that he says he has to leave. When I ask him what the secret to his tireless and prolific life is, Bob says, "Just keep breathing." He smiles and says goodbye before vanishing like a dream.

Left to wander my way out of Watermill, I visit the silent stones standing in the woods before stepping through the maze of moving grass. Walking taller, I find myself with a wider awareness, receiving and transmitting all the vibrations that are shared between nature and man. I feel on the cusp of a great creative expansion where the recreation of the human spirit is all.

Robert Wilson at time of interview, summer 2006 at Watermill. Photo by J. Price.

TWILIGHT ON THE LOWER EAST SIDE

or The Case of the Stanton Street Synagogue

April 14, 1997

To whom it may concern,

I am the head Rabbi of the Stanton Street Synagogue. I believe that there are many good and positive things happening at the 8th St. Shul. Our Synagogues must remain open so that Jews have a place to pray and learn. This is the spirit of these holy places. ... Wherever there is good work being done it must continue. We cannot let our shuls disappear. We all must work together for the common good of Jews and all Mankind.

Very Truly Yours,

Rabbi Joseph Singer

GOD IS TIMING.

The above letter was written by the rabbi of the Stanton Street Synagogue and included in the support papers in the failed court battle to save the 8th Street Shul from being sold in 1997. In the summer of 2000, its author, Rabbi Joseph Singer, met with a Jesuit priest named Brother Rick Curry who heads the National Theatre for the Handicapped and who was looking to purchase the Stanton Street Synagogue from the Rabbi for 1.2 million dollars.

In January of 1998 I was hanging out on Stanton Street between Clinton and Attorney when an older gentleman ran up to me, pulled at my elbow and asked me in a word, "AreyouJewish?" I replied in the affirmative, and the man took me across the street and down into the Shul of the Stanton Street Synagogue to make minyan.

A minyan is a gathering of at least 10 Jewish men over the age of 18.

Before I got two feet into what seemed like 1955 - or was it 1915 - I was welcomed graciously by the many members of the house. Each person who approached me seemed to be inches shorter than the one before, and every one graciously offered me a cup of coffee. I have since learned to agree to the cup of Folgers-instant when it is first offered, if only to save everyone all the fuss. Soon one gentleman was searching for a yarmulke for me and another went looking for a prayer book with English translation. As soon as I was settled, the women left the shul, and I, along with eleven other men, began the twilight prayer. Some stood, some sat, some read, some talked about other things. Rabbi Singer sang.

I found an awakening in the music and chants of the mariv prayers, even though I don't know how to read or speak Hebrew. There is something lost inside me that gets water when I hear Jewish prayers sung. The more I am with the music the closer I get to my true self, the one I have never had the chance to meet. I didn't know the song was lost until I heard it.

The sun went down outside on the Lower East Side, turning the streets that blue that carries me on the crest of weeping. Somewhere between jubilant and sorrowful, between God and the world down here.

Over the next couple of years, I returned occasionally to the Stanton Street Shul, especially on High Holidays. It became my sole place of worship.

In the first months of the year 2000 I began seeing flyers around with a banner headline that read: "Help Save Our Synagogue." After a few months I buckled and called the number on the flyer. I reached the home of Ms. Iris Blutreich who said she was glad to get my call and wanted to meet with me as soon as possible. We made a date to meet at the synagogue.

I've learned a couple of things so far in my life, and one of them is simply: God is timing. The date was May 15, 2001.

Iris and I met on the corner and walked to the synagogue to find that we were unable to enter. The locks had been changed and a note was put on the door by Feldman Realty, a Brooklyn company, which read:

"Anyone breaking in and entering the synagogue will be considered trespassing and will be prosecuted to the full extent of the law."

Iris called Feldman Realty and was told that a lawyer by the name of Eliot Lauer had a letter from the Attorney General's office permitting them to break into the synagogue and change the locks. She then called Assistant Attorney General Carl Di Stefano, who works at the Charities Bureau.

Mr. Di Stefano said that his office had given no such permission. He said further that the Attorney General's office was told a board voted to sell the shul. He said that he was informed that the "dissident congregants" are the ones who first changed the locks. He strongly recommended that the locks not be cut again, and that Benjamin "Benny" Sauerhaft, the president of the congregation, should go through Feldman Realty to get a key.

He also said that he left a message for Eliot Lauer, Singer's lawyer, about what had happened and asked him to expedite the process of getting a key to the congregation. Mr. Lauer hadn't returned the phone call yet.

After this conversation, I went back to the synagogue to watch the locks being cut and changed again.

33

THE STORY SO FAR

Iris gave me a briefing on all that I had missed up until that point. Around the beginning of 2001 congregants were informed that Rabbi Singer was selling the shul because, in his words, there were people who read the prayers out of sync, came late to services and were only there to eat. He said he was becoming too old and feeble to walk to Stanton Street and urged congregants to move with him to the Litovisker Synagogue on Delancey and Columbia Street. Before Purim Rabbi Singer plastered signs on the walls of the synagogue telling people not to come back. These signs were taken down by congregants and immediately replaced by Rabbi Singer, who insisted that the synagogue was going to be closed after Purim.

In the dead of night, after Purim, Rabbi Singer and his family removed two Sefer Torahs (valued at $80,000) and many Art Scroll Siddurim (prayer books) and Chumashes (Bibles). They also took the refrigerator, the freezer and some chairs. Congregants were turned away when they tried to inform the 7th Precinct of the theft.

Iris then asked Ms. Zuckerman, an official at the Attorney General's office, to tell her the names of the board members listed in the vote to sell the Shul. Iris attested that most were members of Rabbi Singer's family, none of whom were voted for by the congregation. According to Ben Sauerhaft the people listed weren't members of the shul, nor had they contributed to the synagogue in any way. They were "outsiders."

Iris pointed me to an article written on March 30, 2001, by Jonathon Mark, an editor at *The Jewish Week* that began, "The small and obscure Stanton Street shul on the Lower East Side seems an unlikely place for Jewish legal history to be made, but that shul may force a judge to decide: who owns a shul divided against itself?"

He quotes Rabbi Singer, who says, "There's nobody left. The board and myself, together, want to sell the shul." Mark continues, "Who'll get the money from the sale? Charity, Rabbi Singer said, 'but they may give me, too, something.'"

Mark goes on, "The shul adversaries appealed to a rabbinical court, but the head of the court, Rabbi David Feinstein, ruled that it was fine to sell if the money stays in the community, where he runs a yeshiva, Mesivta Tifereth Jerusalem. Rabbi Singer told *The Jewish Week* that Rabbi Feinstein's yeshiva would, indeed, share in the real estate deal."

Mark also quotes Joel Kaplan, director of the United Jewish Council, who describes Rabbi Singer as "a beloved personality. I don't see the congregation being able to support the shul at this point. Under the circumstances, the sale should be concluded."

The article goes on, "The Jewish Community Relations Council's David Pollack explained that as large Orthodox families are unable to find large enough apartments, they move out of the neighborhood, leaving mostly the young, transient or elderly."

In a letter dated March 13, 2001, Iris writes passionately to Mr. Di Stefano asking, "Who gives [Singer] the right to sell something that is not his? Why doesn't he sell the Brooklyn

Bridge too?" She also asks, "If Catherine Baecher [Singer's lawyer] is a lawyer, can't she be disbarred for being a party to a fraud that involved helping the Singers sell property that they don't own?" She concludes, "As Americans we value the laws of the land. We look to the protections that they give us so that we may conduct our affairs tranquilly. We expect that your office will uphold these laws which are the only protection every citizen can have against chaos. Laws without the will of officials to enforce them are the beginning of the end of everything that Americans cherish. Will anyone then start to rob and maim knowing that government no longer cares?"

THINGS BETTER LEFT UNSAID

In New York we are given the gift of anonymity. Over the next few months, I talked with some of the key players in our story as a concerned congregant. Some revealed things to me without fully realizing or caring who I was.

I spoke with Mr. Di Stefano on the afternoon of May 16 and asked him if he was aware of any contract of sale. He replied, "Yes there IS a contract, but it is null until it is agreed to by the Supreme Court, and no one has applied to the Supreme Court". He understood that there had been "efforts at mediation with David Pollock of the Jewish Community Relations Council" (JCRC). The JCRC's mission is to be "the voice of the Jewish Community to protect and defend Jewish interests."

A couple of days later I spoke with David Pollock, the JCRC's Associate Executive Director and Director, Government Relations. Pollock immediately painted a metaphoric picture for me. "What we were dealing with was a parent/child relationship", he said. Rabbi Singer was the parent in his scenario. And the question he posed was, Has the child grown up enough to be on its own?

If the congregation could guarantee the Rabbi's pension, then the Rabbi would stop the sale of the synagogue, he continued. "That would go far," he said simply. "You don't have to find $300,000 immediately." I asked if that was the amount that Rabbi Singer would receive if the sale went through for 1.2 million, and he replied: Yes. He said he worked that out to $18,000 a year, and that Mr. Lauer, Singer's lawyer, was up-ing that number to $25,000. If there were a "guaranteed funding stream, it would go a long way to solving this."

I called Brother Curry on May 24 while he was working in Maine. I told him that there was still a congregation of worshippers at the synagogue he wished to buy. He said that he had a contract and that he was bound to it. He signed it one year and two weeks ago, he said. One week prior to that he had read an ad in a real estate magazine and contacted Rabbi Singer. He said that he had met with Rabbi Singer on more than one occasion and that the business dealings had been with him. He said they had a signed contract and now he was waiting for the deal to get "unstuck." It was not a personal thing for him, he said; he was simply bound by a contract and his duty to his Board of Trustees and his disabled students.

I contacted Mr. Spitzer's office on July 5 by e-mail, asking, "What knowledge of the sale of the Stanton Street Synagogue do you have? What is your position?"

On July 17 a woman named Jessica called from Mr. Spitzer's office. She said that she had double-checked with the Charities Bureau, which oversees religious and other non-profit organizations, before calling me, and that they had said that the case had been "stagnant for a couple of months now" and that the synagogue was "not being sold." She said that a Mr. Avischick, an attorney at the Charities Bureau, told her this. She said according to him the United Jewish Council led by Joel Kaplan ("he's been amazing") was responsible for stopping the sale "a couple of months ago." The word from Kaplan was that the sale was becoming "too expensive for the Singer family."

I immediately called up Brother Curry with the good news. I told him that the Attorney General's office had informed me that the sale was off. He said he had heard no claim of that sort and that he was moving forward with the sale and moreover he believed that the Shul was rightly his.

I spoke with Carl Di Stefano on July 24, 2001. He said that to his knowledge the lawyers were in the process of deciding. He said he had talked to Avischick, who denied the statements attributed to him by Jessica in Mr. Spitzer's office. No further explanation was given.

I couldn't get Joel Kaplan on the phone, but I did get back in touch with Mr. Pollock. On July 30, 2001, David Pollock said that the congregants had to decide what to do, and then we could give him a call. "More than that," he said, "the JCRC are keeping their hands off."

Because it looked like we were going to have to put up a fight in court and didn't have a lawyer, I tried to find the shul some legal advice. I called the New York Legal Assistance Group on the recommendation of the Jewish Information and Referral Service. I talked with Ms. Constance Carden, who was given the task of investigating our case in order to determine whether the firm could advise us. She said that she had talked to a lawyer with the JCRC, Marsha Eisenberg, with David Pollock in the room, and that Ms. Eisenberg had said that there was no problem, because the case had not gone to court.

I told the entire story to Ms. Carden, and she recommended that everyone continue to pray at the shul until the case went to court. At that time, she said, I should call on Marsha Eisenberg to find us a lawyer who could help. I explained to Ms. Carden that Ms. Eisenberg's organization would get a cut from the sale and that they had every intention on working toward selling what wasn't theirs. Ms. Carden did not change her position. She took diligent notes of our conversation, never contradicting my allegations that what was being done was illegal and that no one was doing anything about it.

JUDGE LIPPMAN'S COURT

We found help in a Groucho-like lawyer named Brian Burstin. He was sent by angels, as they say, via Iris. He took on our case with verve and a healthy dose of humor.

The congregation arrived at Judge Robert Lippman's courtroom at 9:30am on November 12. There weren't enough chairs for everyone. After an hour of waiting our case was heard. Brian Burstin, alongside Carl Di Stefano, stood beside Rabbi Singer's goateed lawyer to argue the case.

From the start Judge Lippman seemed quick to dismiss the claim of the assembled congregants. He took no time or effort to learn any of the truth behind the situation, hearing only Singer's "arguments." Singer's goateed lawyer spewed lies and distorted accounts of what had gone on since "the vote" and sale in June of 2000.

Judge Lippman saw us as trying to stop a good Rabbi from making some money off of unused property. He asked if the congregants were willing or able to pay the 1.2 million dollars that had been offered for the synagogue. He belittled the number of congregants in attendance as "these 7 or 8 people," prompting the assembled congregation of twenty-five or so to stand up (though standing was not allowed in the courtroom) to show themselves.

The Judge asked for everyone to return to the court on November 16 to hold an evidentiary hearing in order to establish ownership of the shul. On that day a frustrated Brother Curry had his lawyers bow out of the sale. Brother Curry had waited long enough and the posters that Iris made and put up around the neighborhood weren't flattering either. The posters had a picture of Brother Curry on it with the headline, "Don't let this man take our synagogue." Iris knew Brother Curry wasn't the real culprit but was fighting by any means necessary.

Before Singer's lawyer could get out of the courtroom, Judge Lippman ordered the family to return both Torah scrolls to the synagogue immediately. The Singer family returned the Torah scrolls two weeks late.

MEANWHILE, AT THE SHUL

In 1913, a man named Max Kramer purchased property at 180 Stanton Street and founded the synagogue, then known as Congregation B'nai Jacob Anschei Brzezan. The synagogue has been in continuous use since its inception. The congregation was listed in 1917, in the Jewish Communal Register, as having 135 members and a 400-seat capacity.

According to the Register, the Lower East Side used to be filled with more than 400 permanent synagogues upholding Jewish traditions and the hope for the future of Judaism in America. Whether orthodox, conservative or reform, all New York Jews were obligated to build houses of worship and Jewish education. This was their inheritance from the Old World.

"Establishing a synagogue or being affiliated with one was not considered a matter of option. It was an accepted principle that whenever there were ten Jews, they were in duty bound to form themselves into a congregation, and to carry on all the customary Jewish communal activities." (Jewish Communal Register, 1917)

It must be true that during the height of the Jewry in New York the Lower East Side was the closest resemblance to the shtetls that they had moved away from, in numbers alone. Communal gathering was the only way to survive. Jews needed each other in order to find the way into the American diaspora and the Lower East Side was the dock-of-entry. In time, hundreds of thousands of first-generation American jews moved up and out the city, leaving the truly eccentric Jews who actually liked life in the City.

About fifteen synagogues remain in the neighborhood while 400 or so synagogues have faded into history. We are at the end of history now, the end of days, the twilight

Check out that new townhouse on East 1st Street between Avenue A and 1st Avenue that used to be a synagogue. Or walk down Pike Street and find the Buddhist temple/bookstore/residence that used to be the glorious Pike Street Synagogue. Or if you find yourself on East 8th Street between Avenues B and C you'll see the empty shell that used to be the 8th Street Shul. Each of these synagogues were a haven for Jews and anyone else those Jews could help.

These synagogues were welcome mats in a world that required more and more membership. They were places to gather at, to be with others, to learn and heighten awareness. A smile or at least a nod of appreciation is all you needed to get in the door.

Same is true of the Stanton Street Synagogue. It continues to be a warm, welcoming place where people can gather to pray, nosh a little and talk about what is going on in the neighborhood and the rest of the world.

OPENING THE WINDOWS AND THE DOORS

On October 15th of this year the congregants were called back to the courthouse downtown to hold the evidentiary hearing that was still necessary to settle who had the right to decide the fate of the synagogue. Judge Lippman had appointed, for reasons unknown, Judge Martin Evans to resolve the case.

Judge Evans, who had been in retirement, has the honorable distinction of having decided a case that set a standard in religious corporate law (Sup. Ct. N.Y. County 1980). It's called the Kroth decision, and it sets out the procedure by which the courts can determine voting members and boards of directors in these ownership cases.

I arrived during recess on the second day of court. I took a chair in the back next to the door and got caught up on what I had missed. Apparently, Rabbi Singer had been on the stand during the first half of the day mumbling through most of his testimony. Singer's new lawyers had apparently tried to invalidate the Orthodoxy of the members of the Stanton Street Synagogue.

Soon after I got the rundown, Rabbi Singer came back from recess.

When I first started living in the neighborhood, I heard great things about Rabbi Singer. Truthfully the first time I heard of the Stanton Street Synagogue, it was referred to as "Rabbi Singer's." Though I could never really understand a word he said, he always struck me as a pious and holy man. Now after many months filled with dismay over his actions to sell the shul, I found his presence subtly shocking.

During the recess, he took the empty seat next to mine and began talking with Iris's daughter, Ahna, who was to his right. For a while he turned his back to me carrying on a conversation about Ahna's education. Then Rabbi Singer asked her if I was her boyfriend. She told him he ought to ask me who I was.

He turned to me, and before he could say a word, I showed him the letter he had authored in support of the 8th Street Shul. I read the entire letter to him and asked him whether he knew the signature at the bottom as his own. He didn't respond. I then asked him all the questions that I had inside me. In this world, where Jews are traditionally disliked, why are we fighting each other, when we need to be supportive and understanding? How could he be responsible for selling the synagogue? Furthermore, I expressed how sad and disillusioned I had become during the fight for the Shul. He listened to everything I said and his response was, "How old are you?"

Then he asked me where my yarmulke was. I told him that I didn't wear one every day and that I wasn't going to pretend I did for the purpose of the court, a court that I didn't want to be attending. Soon Rabbi Singer took off his own yarmulke and placed it on my head. I wore it throughout the rest of the day's proceedings, which consisted primarily of Ben Sauerhaft's testimony.

When court was adjourned, Rabbi Singer's son-in-law, Abe Schwarzman, came up to me and demanded, "Will you please give my father back his yarmulke?" I told him that I was on my way to do just that. He then said to Rabbi Singer under his breath, "Giving him your yarmulke is like putting it in the trash." I was deeply offended, and I told him as much. He replied, "Oh, you would wear it?" I said, "I'd be honored to wear the Rabbi's yarmulke," as I handed it back to Rabbi Singer and thanked him for lending it to me.

On Tuesday October 22, 2002, we were called back to court to continue the hearing at 2pm. (If you don't see the magic in those numbers, you ain't gonna.) I arrived right on time to pass our lawyer, Mr. Burstin, on the pay phone. His colleague Mr. Jonathon Boyarin told me that they were making phone calls that they didn't want to make, but the Judge had asked them to. Certainly, something was up.

I arrived onto the fourth floor of 80 Center Street and ducked into the bathroom. Iris's husband, Bruce, was there. During all of the court proceedings, Bruce and I analyzed the

39

situation outside of earshot of others. He told me that nothing was happening in the courtroom, everyone was whispering outside. As we walked down the hallway past Singer's family and lawyers, I acknowledged each of them with a "good day."

For the second time I took a seat behind and to the left of the Judge's desk. Ms. Goldman approached me quickly. Ms. Goldman is a Hasidic woman from Borough Park who looks like Emma Goldman reincarnated though she had never heard of Emma. She was sent direct from the Rebbe King Moschiach, the Borough Hall Rebbe who proselytizes in New York City on High Holidays, to observe the proceedings. Ms. Goldman told me when we first met on October 15th that the Rebbe was extraordinarily upset about what had been going on with the attempted sale of the Shul.

We sat by the windows and she whispered that it was the 22nd at 2pm and she was exhilarated. Something great was happening and we didn't have anything to do but watch. Ms. Goldman came onto the scene in time to witness history being made as the synagogue's continued life was granted.

Iris came over to turn on the fan. Ms. Goldman and I opened the windows and pulled up the shades. We waited in the quiet room with the light reflecting in. All the congregants in attendance wore pins that read "Save Our Shul" with a picture of the synagogue on it. It was another stroke of Iris' constant battle.

At no time during the last year and a half had Iris ever stopped. She was always writing the letters, faxing the faxes, making the posters, putting them up, editing videos, and showing them on Manhattan Neighborhood Network (MNN). All the while, with the same passion, she was making sure that there was always a good spread of food at the Shul and that the garden out front on Stanton Street was watered and cared for.

All the lawyers and family came back into the room. When everyone settled, Judge Evans, with his hands folded in his lap, said simply, "All claims have been resolved. Go in peace."

The family skirted out with their lawyers as the congregation started whispering questions to Brian. He explained that the Judge had "dismissed with prejudice," which meant that the Singer family could never try to claim ownership of the Stanton Street Synagogue again. A definitive and triumphant decision.

Out of court Rabbi Singer's lawyers made a deal for the Rabbi and his family to go away for the sum of $24,000 over the next three years. The money will be paid to him by an outside benefactor. No responsibility to pay is laid on the synagogue. The congregants were never given an opportunity to be involved in any deal, but apparently Judge Evans, from the beginning of the proceedings, pushed for a quiet settlement that was agreeable to all.

Out on the steps of the court building we stood in the sunlight waiting for Benny, who stayed behind to thank the Judge. The congregants all wished each other heartfelt Mazel Tovs. Some cried happy exhausted tears. We stood there dizzy and exalted on an unexpectedly beautiful day. Benny came out and told us that Judge Evans apparently said to him, "You deserve to have the synagogue." Benny kissed the Judge on his forehead.

VULTURES STILL OVERHEAD

This article is just scratching the surface, a bubble-gum story compared to what's really going on.

In Geoffrey Gray's *Village Voice* article ("Crisis of Faith" May 29, 2001) he quotes Abe Schwarzman saying, "It's not really a synagogue. Even if these people do breathe some life into the synagogue in the next couple of months, it will just be artificial resuscitation. Whether it be six months or a year, I don't know. But it cannot exist."

Days after the October 22nd decision, Iris sent me a fax with the headline "Synagogue Saved! Be vigilant!" When I talked with her she told me a old camp story of hers. The moral was: never sleep while others were awake.

Truth is, the synagogue may have won this time, but it's not over. Rabbi Singer was a patsy, suckered into the scheme because of the promise of a big payout. He was the front man to Brother Curry, and the United Jewish Council and the Jewish Community Relations Council pushed it along, waited in the wings and hoped for the best.

And these vultures are still out there quick and ready to sell the soul of our neighborhood. They're ready to live in a vacuum, with a unified voice, community influence and lots of money for the few. There is no end in sight.

If Rabbi Singer would have gotten $300,000 in the 1.2-million-dollar deal with Brother Curry, where would the rest of the money have gone? The UJC and the JCRC among others would have been in control of dividing up the money. This much we know.

Where have all the synagogues gone? Who has profited from those real estate deals? They have been caught threatening the congregants, locking them out, stealing their Torahs, and sending the whole lot of them through the courts and the papers, for nothing more than money. These same "organizations" are now at the front door with the keys.

During the early months of 2002 the Stanton Street Synagogue held elections for their new board. Most of the regular congregant members came to vote, but most were unable to actually take on any volunteer post. In turn, some people were elected to the board whose true affiliations are suspect.

Board members had a tremendous influence in the synagogue getting landmark status in August of this year. With a benefit at the Angel Orensanz Synagogue the synagogue raised over $20,000 for the shul. $10,000 went directly to an architectural assessment and $3,000 went to Holly Kaye Executive Director of the Lower East Side Conservancy, who wrote the application. In August the Stanton Street Synagogue received the illustrious title of Landmark of Historical Significance. What next? The Conservancy will probably include the Stanton Street Synagogue on their walking tours. Just recently, the synagogue was included in their on-line map of Lower East Side.

The Conservancy, created in 1998, has a stunning mission statement, which reads: "Our mission is the preservation and promotion of Jewish culture on New York's Lower East Side, from the nostalgic 'old' neighborhood of a century ago to the vibrant and growing Jewish community of today." The Conservancy was formed with the sponsorship of the United Jewish Council of the Lower East Side, Inc. The executive director, Joel Kaplan of the UJC, was quoted in the Jewish Week's summing-up article of the Stanton Street Synagogue case ("Shul Keeps Its Spirit" by Eric Greenberg 11/01/2002) saying, "I think we're pleased that the shul will continue. Hopefully the future of the shul is settled." This is the same Joel Kaplan who threatened to personally sue any congregant who got in the way of the sale of the synagogue.

What does he mean by "I think we're pleased ..." or "Hopefully"?

Ever since the synagogue settled its score with Rabbi Singer, the congregants have been engaged in finding a new rabbi and making the necessary repairs to the building. There's a hole in the roof, three aged skylights, and a fire-escape that needs to be replaced. Iris took it upon herself to find estimates from neighborhood people who are willing to do the work at a low cost. She estimates that the synagogue needs $26,000 to do all the work.

The estimate that the board came up with is $136,000. They say the synagogue needs an $80,000 loan in order to do the repairs – a loan the synagogue could never pay back.

The real story that nobody wants to talk about, is the conflict between property value and the value of continued prayer. The great work of profiting off of the synagogues of yesterday is already over. The work is done. It's business as usual. This has been going on in New York since its first developer, its first lawyer, its first court.

I recently heard that the Conservancy was given keys. They seek a shul that will be pristine and tourist-friendly, or at least more valuable on the market. Unfortunately, with more tourists comes more estrangement of all the beautiful souls of the synagogue that give their time to God and their labor in prayer.

The Stanton Street Synagogue is one of the last remaining shuls that gets by on nothing more than generosity of spirit, individuality, and righteous off-beat song. If they sell the Shul from the inside, then they will have thrown the last log on the pyre. And the dark days of heartless real estate and greed will continue to burn.

Where there should be compassion and support, there is only derision and separatism in the prattle and practice of philistines. This fight is one among many that has been fought throughout our history. The Stanton Street Synagogue won, for now. Who will be there tomorrow?

Iris Blutreich

Members of Stanton Street Shul

43

IT'S NOT A SAFE SPACE BUT IT'S WHERE WE LIVE

LISTENING TO STEW AND THE NEGRO PROBLEM'S *NOTES OF A NATIVE SONG* AND *THE TOTAL BENT*

It's rare when a new album comes out that affects us so deeply that we are impelled to listen to it repeatedly and write down its lyrics. That's what happens with Stew and the Negro Problem's two fresh cast albums, *Notes of a Native Song* and *The Total Bent*. No stage production is necessary to enjoy these musical explorations—with insightful poetry, slammin' music, and great performers, something indelible and precious is created.

After Stew's audacious *Passing Strange* earned him a Tony Award for Best Book, he followed it up with a couple of shows that continue to disrupt the status quo. Here is music that awakens those who are unconscious and enlivens those who want to "stretch their definition of funky." Stew's songs are riddled with revelations about love, the world, and the struggles of being black in America.

Notes of a Native Song begins without prologue or overture stepping directly into a dialogue with the audience and inviting us on a journey that could change our point of view.

Say Harlem girl

With your stress and your curl

Would you like to change worlds

and accompany me... to Baldwin Country?

Native Song is rooted in the wisdom and life of James Baldwin but it's not a biographical musical, rather it's a thoughtful introduction to Baldwin's path toward social awareness and personal truth. The show shakes our shoulders, trying to snap us out of our national amnesia. Pounding drums and wailing strings smash urgently under the thought:

And then you remember, you try to remember

You hope you remember

Did you forget to remember?

Do you know how to remember?

The eclectic music travels from punk to rock to transcendental soundscapes and is decidedly not musical theatre. Both albums topple boundaries and transport us to a place where we can hear each another. Within each song, which exist somewhere between our ears, a whispered message comes through of some secret information or a simple revelation. "Baldwin Country," the opening song, ends with:

When love meets truth

There's a lot to forgive

It's not a safe space

But it's where we live. ...

The journey of *Native Song* is a determined one and something we should undertake together. Even with Stew's wicked and ruthless sense of humor there is recognition and understanding. Heidi Rodewald's sly-toned back-up vocals and bass anchor the music, balancing the angelic with the mischievous. Looking around "Florida," the scene of Trayvon Martin's murder and his killer's acquittal, the scene of "hangin' chads and lynchin' boys," Stew gives it up for the People's Republic of Brooklyn.

When I turn into an old Jew, I will not retire in you

I'm staying in Brooklyn where the struggle is best

It don't matter if the weather is great

if I have to wear a bulletproof vest.

Heidi sings the refrain on this one, "Florida, Florida you kill me." But in Brooklyn we live and do what we do because we can. Brooklynites make art imbued it with authenticity, intuition, and spunk.

These are qualities that Vondie Curtis Hall, who plays the character Joe Roy, brings to the elder preacher in *The Total Bent* with a sultry commanding voice, he confronts us with honesty, righteousness, and venom. When *The Total Bent* begins our jaw drops to the floor, as Stew's chutzpah knows no bounds.

I did some fucked up shit but he forgot about it

That's why he's Jesus and you're not whitey

45

There's no room for complacency. This shocking beginning is followed by the sweet vibrancy of Ato Blankson-Wood's Marty Roy, Joe's musician son, who is trying to connect with his audience without God. His refrain echoes, "I'm so black and blue baby."

The voices, words, and music are enough to make us know justice and peace. It's no wonder that the Great White Way didn't herald the second coming of Stew with *The Total Bent* because it lands a solid blow to the establishment through its brazen and direct confrontation.

Shut up and get back on the bus and take a back seat with a smile

Shut up and stop makin' a fuss and suffer your oppression in style. ...

Don't expect everything tied up neatly. We are left with the knowledge that the fear of love might be what is perpetuating our alienation. If we listen carefully and address each other and ourselves honestly then we might be able to break out of these dark times. Indeed, with *Notes of a Native Song* and *The Total Bent* we take a step forward toward empathy and understanding.

Stew's *Native Song* at the Curran Theater. Photo courtesy of Earl Dax.

RIDING UNTIL WE GET THERE

waging peace in NYC

For eight days I rode my bike with a big PEACE sign on the back wearing an upside-down American flag as a cape. I must have clocked over a hundred miles during the convention randomly riding in circles around midtown confronting people, fellow protestors and the Republicans.

Most of the time when I made eye contact, I held up my two-fingered peace sign and quietly waited for a response. When I got a positive sign back it felt as if we had made an agreement that we will both act to restore peace and will live peacefully now in order to see peace in the future.

The majority of the people did not respond or would curse at me. My only wish is that they had to think about their negative response as they saw the word PEACE on the back of my bike. What do they want? War? Hopefully a seed of doubt was planted.

From time to time, I sang my own Passover song, "Get Out of Egypt". The lyrics include: "Bush lied, we cried. The news said he was right. The Constitution has died. So, get out and shout tonight." Sometimes I sang "Here Comes the Sun" with one word changed in the opening lyrics: "Little darling, it seems like years since PEACE has been here."

Most of the younger cops nodded their support or raised their hands with a thumbs up or a peace sign themselves. Fortunately, no officers forced me to stop as long as I kept the flow and didn't get in the way. My heart goes out to all those patriots who were arrested, and their bikes confiscated.

The fluidity and freedom of my bike enabled me to be anywhere and everywhere during the demonstrations. I was able to join the Green Dragon's Paul Revere ride announcing, "The Republicans are coming!" and I was one of the 5,000 bikes in the Critical Mass ride. I walked my bike in the United for Peace and Justice march and rode all over the city during the August 31st day of direct actions.

I saw a live board game of American Oligopoly that had our present Big Business political landscape represented and the Bush crew playing the Kerry party. I also caught the Eyes Wide Open installation in Central Park with boots and shoes representing the troops and civilians killed in Iraq.

On the last night of the convention my bike ride rant boiled down to, "Hey delegates, news flash: Bush is lying to you!" One Republican man mouthed quietly to me that he knew Bush was lying, to which I said, "When you go in your voting booth you don't have to vote for him." Before popping into a cab, he whispered, "I'm not."

I'm writing this down not for self-congratulation but in the hopes of inspiring other bikers to devise their own signs and songs. Even though the convention is over, it is imperative that we continue our direct confrontation as often as possible. Let's go to the tourist traps in the city and engage those Americans that need to reconsider their vote and where they place their support.

The work isn't over when we have so far to go. Let's divide and conquer.

Power to the peaceful.

Dated September 5, 2004

Wally in front of the New York Public Library after it was shut down by police during the Republican National Convention in New York City, August 2004.

Photo by A. P. Ferrara.

BACKGAMMON RULES

Backgammon is about making choices that are risky or safe, provocative, or defensive, an act of listening and observing the potential in every moment, doing the best with what you have. Like in theatre, the play becomes an opportunity to wrestle one's ego with the random moment. Elliot and I came up with our own rules:

1. Play without fear or greed. (You'll lose the game with either one.)
2. Easily ask for what you want to see. (The dice doesn't hear you when you're screaming.)
3. Discretion is the better part of valor. (If you must attack, be discreet.)

REMEMBER: You are the servant of chance, so ... ROLL THE DICE!

Elliot Blum

Backgammon is played on a board with 24 triangles, called points, which are divided into four quadrants. The centuries-old two-player game features fifteen checkers whose aim are to move from their starting point to their home and eventually off the board.

The movement of the checkers is determined by the roll of two dice. Each triangle is called a **point**. The points function as spaces on the board, along which players' pieces move, based on the roll of the dice.

If a player has more than one piece on a point, then it is a **block** where their opponent can't land on. If a piece is left alone on a point, then they are vulnerable to being **hit** and sent to the bar, the central spine of the backgammon board. We scored our games like a tennis match, best of for each set, and match. A game is worth one point. A "gammon" is when your opponent hasn't taken any pieces off the board and is worth two points. If your opponent leaves a piece in your 'home' when you're all off, that's a "backgammon" worth three points.

THE BACKGAMMON BOOKS record over 1,000 games

between Wally (aka Doublé) and his father-in-love, Elliot Blum (aka Big E). After each game they recorded the wisdom that was revealed, fully enjoying the frivolity, the volatility, and the deep trawling that came with the play. Here are excerpts:

Reflections
        maybe that's what
the game of chances
        is a mystery of
shifting perspectives
        where are we now
beyond the philosophy and cup shaking
        we transcend into a clear
reflection of each other
        just as we are
no more competition on the long leg of time
        after these many years
we are blissed and blessed
        to see inside ourselves and each other

        "What goes around, comes around
        What comes around, goes around …"

There is definitely an energy coursing through our cups – a celestial delight, someone is laughing somewhere

Big E's always friggin' surprised

One friggin' unnecessary risk and all will be lost – BLUM GAMMONS

It was in Big E's bones, one of the most amazing games, back and forth

Big E hits six times in a row with the 3/5 double hit – no game for Wally, it's a GAMMON BLUM "it's a little spooky"

Nighttime - the moon shines on the pond like the Eiffel Tower

Double 6s at the right time can answer all questions quickly, Big E takes it
a Pyrrhic victory

Crazy game Big E gets the 6s again which makes all the flim flam moot   BLUM GAMMONS

Big E unleashes the doubles, Wally leaves two on
What can we say? Reset.
Blum finishes with 6s
As vivid as a nightmare he rolls the 5 when Wally had a gammon goin' easy he leaves three and gives up the game
I bet the odds and not the gut … live and learn

It feels like *Rocky* in the twelfth round sluggin' away, Wally takes it

Wally finishes with 4s after a game with three double sixes and Wally all off before any of Big E's ten men are in his home GAMMON WALLY

Wow major change in direction
Wally has the dice - and the dice have him

Match point was in Wally's cup … he remained as calm as the man who gets to decapitate the cow
Double 6s again brought Big E to his knees, the rest was a steady beating til the end
a volatile match
stunning for its possessiveness

HARD KNOCK SUMMER 2013

Wally remains calm throughout ... know the potential of every moment and never be discouraged

magic is in the air

WINTER 2013
Golly god damn

Wally had eight men out before getting hit and losing with two pips
Blum is back in Brooklyn
Two sets of doubles from Big E, 5s finish

Big E keeps slapping him down
Wally can't really catch a break
held his 6s once but it was too little too late
great gaming

How did he do it?!
Wally had the edge, fish in the barrel, but no
Big E slaps and goes, finishes with 6s

Come on! Wally finishes with 6s

Slugfest! Fightin' to the finish
Wally gets 6s to get the game

I left a man alone in his house
he said, "that man will never see the light of day" And I stood on the bar as Big E takes off eight men

"Backgammon – it ain't about the dice."

Big E looking at Gammon or Backgammon
He kissed himself to death

Wally comes around and takes it

"We've got a gammon here ..." Wally opened his arrogant mouth and only gets a game

52

Wally thought he had it but
No – we are at war with the ego

Wally takes the game
Our dog Sid's eventual passing is
overshadowing ...

SPRING 2014
The only teacher is a good question.

A ballet to begin
a no-hitter for a long while
then a bit of a 3-1 street fight
Wally takes first blood

e Double Trouble, 5s 6s and finishing with 3s
nice dice - need every one
Wally kept quiet and took the GAMMON
When he's hot, he's hot

Holy moly
Has ever a man used all 4 6s to hit and bring Backgammon back into the realm of possibilities, for a moment, until he moves the 3-2 men out
Sea change
We welcome Mr. Blum
El Habana back into the fray
and the music is good too   GAMMON BLUM

How do extraterrestrials influence the dice? The spin, the landing ...
How could those Double 2s be random, when they were inevitable?

Big E misplays his snake eyes, gives up the GAMMON (Wally!),
when all his men were home
–
Big E comes to the new match giving it up for fun
leaves 5 men in the backfield
Wally finishes with 6s and a GAMMON
–
Ending with 5s Wally makes magic with Big E
the things we've seen - the possibilities

Wow! The Blum Stratagem succeeds – never seen anything like it
hitting Wally 18 times and stacking his men on the 1,2. He powers his way to a defiant
defeat of Wally GAMMON BLUM

The dice are speaking to us

Wally seemed to come on like horses throwing E to the wall while being mocked by the
bones - but then a shift in the breeze, and Big E flips the tide
throwing Wally onto the bar

and taking back the horse race until Wally slips out of town with 2s and then doubles brought
the game, and our lives, into our cups, both with 3 left on the one, each with a chance

we end this one-pipper in Wally's favor
tie game —   the wrist is back, Big E will not be stopped

Playing on the wild side
we can be crazy together
splendid spring cleaning

Chance isn't in your cup until after one's opponent has rolled
Every roll is an opportunity. The path is the goal.

Photo by Belinda Blum.

54

ADVICE FOR DADDY-DOULAS

Stay by her side as often as possible, palms up, ready for anything.

Give her water as often as possible. Overdo the amount of water intake the last month of pregnancy.

Find a water bottle, with a screw-tight lid and long straw.

Brew large quantities of red raspberry leaf tea (the loose leaf - not the tea bag) and have them available in bottles in the fridge.

Preparing for Big Day

Consider the lighting for your hospital room. Bring white Christmas lights and everyone will be glad you did.

Have music ready to go. Be sure to have soothing music as well as the harder, more rhythmic tunes for the pushing.

Clip her fingernails often around the "due date".

The Big Day

Don't talk so much during labor. Listen.

Scented oils are good to have, spearmint for pep, eucalyptus and lavender to calm her. You can put a dab on her neck or wrists.

Lip balm is very helpful as her lips will get dry often.

Touch her nipples lightly and make-out with her for stimulation and relaxation.

Cutting the cord is the easiest part, just do it.

Have something ready to feed your lady after she's gone through the birth. Slippers and a robe are good to bring too, though pack something you don't care much about as it's a bloody mess.

Berlin street art, 2002

What if?

The soul enters the body right before a person's first breath. Consciousness in the womb is unconscionable. Once the cord is cut there are two people, not before. If this is true, then our soul could have chosen or fallen perfectly into this body due to its cosmic makeup, found in its astrological birth chart. Life then might be the opportunity for our light to evolve and expand so that when we leave this three-dimensional reality, we might enter a higher dimension, perhaps not on this planet.

All sentient extraterrestrial neighbors envy our oceans, our biodiversity, and our chocolate. Earth is special, she makes what she makes. It's different everywhere else. No other Goldilocks planet out there, amongst the trillions of other habitable planets, have the peanut butter cup, but I bet they have theatre.

I don't think our spirits are waiting in line to get in – I think there's a great miasma of light and it goes and flows where it wants to go freely, sometimes for no reason at all.

How to Fly in Manhattan:
a biker's guide

Only one person is necessary to play,

but you need the city to survive.

FORWARD

The truth of G-d's perfect timing is clearest of all when I ride within the fabric and rhythm of this City.

Each day in Manhattan, I organize my list of things to do, and devise in my head a geometrical shape that connects the dots. Once I figure out the most economical order of stops, I hop on my bike and let the city guide me from place to place. Down Broadway, around Battery Park, and up the Hudson, or over the Brooklyn Bridge, or best of all, a flight through Central Park. The longer the distance, the closer I come to a new thought. At any hour, rain or shine, all days of the year, I ride. I fly. Sometimes for no reason at all.

When I don't know my destination, I simply follow the green lights. Having faith that I'll know when I have arrived. My feet will never touch the ground before I get there.

And during a flight, Manhattan plays like an echo chamber or a mimic that will give back whatever I give out. So, if I yell, New York will yell back, if I smile, it'll smile back even quicker. The city is our mirror, undisturbed, unapologetic, and without hesitation. New Yorker's have a way of call and response, that happens in a breath.

Pedestrians can experience it in a passing taxi on the go, or as they're running for the train. But for the New York City bicyclists, the opportunities for exchange are too numerous to count. With a wink or glance, cars will stop, and pedestrians will make room. Human nature can be observed clearly from these interactions. Everyone is grateful to be seen and acknowledged.

The city can also be a great escape. If I don't fight, the city won't fight back. As long as the pursuit is agreeable, the city will conspire and give space to pass safely. By "agreeable" I mean, saying "Yes!" to all things, at every moment. Go! Always move forward with grace and clarity, finding that opening, for that moment, that will allow safe passage.

It's improvisation. If I hesitate or become arrogant, it could be fatal. Through riding daily, I learn to be generous and to never to look back. Always looking ahead, I deal with what is in front of me, never lose the pace of the pedaling or let my feet touch the ground.

I thought maybe this isn't a bike guide, maybe I'm really writing a biography of my bike and myself. But, No! Doesn't everybody need a "How To", a "Biking in Manhattan for Dummies". I think we need function. No function, no future. These days everything around us must assist us in some way. We need help, we do. Well, "get on your bike and RIDE!"

Manhattan's original name comes from the language of the Indians who enjoyed this island before the first conquering, the Wappinger Confederacy of the Algonquin tribe. They called this island Manah-atin, meaning "island of hills". Yes, Uptown and Downtown refer to more than numbers. The city grid was made to create long runways of perpetual flight. Streets and Avenues. When you cross any Avenue, stop in the middle for a second and look in either direction and you'll be convinced.

The island is not a flat desert or parking lot like Los Angeles or filled with circles like Paris or Rome. It isn't sprawled wide like London, San Francisco, or most other cities. Manhattan Island has got her legs close together. She's tall and thin, a celestial structure of movement. But the heavens are boundless, here we've got the Hudson and East Rivers running on both sides.

Movement on and around this island is what makes that hum, that beat, that pulse, that THING, that gets tourists dizzy when they arrive, that THING that starts Manhattanites marching on the pavement or taking to their bikes. It is Her... Manhattan, island of hills, island of roller coasters, runways, and flight.

Come one, come all - it is the greatest roller coaster in the world. Get the wheels and the wings are free. It may take practice and experience, like any other musical instrument or hobby you might express yourself through, but that is simply time.

The rhythm of this city is a collective gamelan, whose every moment is welcoming to new players. There can never be too many drums. The city is built for thousands of more bikes than there are now.

I've seen pictures of the bike riders in Tokyo. Usually, the photos are of massive groups of bicyclists waiting with cars at an intersection. This sight you will never see in Manhattan. With no time to stop, everyone is in motion. It is a far cry from monotonous. There are variables, tonal shifts, and rhythmic structures that rise and fall with the sun and each new block.

Tonight, the Empire State Building is lit green on top. I ride home in the rain from Chelsea. Perching at Greenwich Street and Sixth Avenue, I see the long and wide river of cars flowing underneath the canopy of Sixth Avenue lights. The Empire State Building stands regal above, reigning over the string of greens, saying simply, "Go!"

This IS the land of Oz; you can go anywhere you want. What you need, Oz will give. And I thought about green some more. Half of the City's heartbeat. The glorious release. Go and let gravity be your only enemy.

58

SUPERBE

Lloyd Morris, in his 1951 book entitled *Incredible New York*, wrote, "the bicycle craze struck New York, and the whole city began pursuing happiness on wheels. Genteel conservatives deplored this new fad and were gratified when the Reverend Asa D. Blackburn, pastor of the Church of Strangers, denounced it from his pulpit. The press commended his sermon: 'You cannot serve God and skylark on a bicycle.' Yet despite his dire warning, the young smart set took to the sort enthusiastically."

Morris continues in the chapter to tell the story of actress Lillian Russell and her friend Marie Dressler cycling through Central Park on weekday mornings. Ms. Russell was a sensation and a scandal. Her bicycle was "entirely gold plated, its mother-of-pearl handlebars bore her monogram in diamonds and emeralds; the hubs and spokes of its wheels were set with many jewels that sparkled in the sun."

Her bicycle is rumored to have been a gift from "Diamond Jim" Brady. It is said that he would ride alongside Ms. Russell in a gold-plated bike with silver spokes and is also credited with driving the first electric carriage down Fifth Avenue, at eleven miles an hour, tying up traffic for two hours.

By 1899, a parade of gasoline or steam "horseless carriages", rode from Fifth Avenue and Thirty-fourth Street to Claremont bypassing Central Park as they were forbidden to enter. Along the parade route, bystanders yelled, "Get a horse!"

In the late seventies, early eighties, I would bike around my condo complex in the furthest corner of the San Fernando Valley in Chatsworth. Even though I don't remember any of their names, I know I named the bikes that I rode. They were pieced together with parts of other bikes: part Schwinn, part Huffy, part Diamondback. When Mom asked me, "Where are you going?", I'd answer simply, "Bikin'." I'd bike with friends or alone, it didn't matter. I loved the speed, the tricks, and jumps. Everything about biking was creative and fast.

I used to run through the school hallways when they were crowded. Jumping and sliding through children walking and talking with their books held close to their chests. I never knocked anyone down. That was the game. How fast and how close could I get to knock some reality into their day, but not enough to stop their flow.

When I was twelve years old, I stopped riding my bike. At the onset of the skateboard and the RTD bus line, I left the bike at home as soon as I started junior high in Northridge, about five miles away from home. The bus and a skateboard became my sole means of transportation. If only I knew then what I know now! How many hours did I waste away at bus stops?! When I got to high school, my friends drove me around. In college, I finally got a car of my own. Alas, ten years and never owned a bike.

I spent most of my college loans on parking tickets in San Diego. With no regard for parking regulations, I liked to drive onto campus and park right next to the classroom. I did it almost every day. A quarter of the time I'd get caught and ticketed. They even came and towed my car from my home while I slept. Coupled with the various moving violations that I couldn't talk my way out of, most of my time, money and energy was spent on my black Pontiac Le Mans.

As soon as I graduated college I moved to Manhattan, West 98th Street, between Broadway and West End. That was in 1994, the ass-end of what used to be New York City.

Soon after my arrival I found employment in the big city and began to "put out the energy" for a bicycle. And after some weeks into Autumn New York's peculiar magic first found me. If you have the fortune to live in New York City you soon realize that through earnest determination, visualization, and patience your wishes begin to manifest themselves on the street. Ask anyone.

On a November night a man I worked with named Edwin, rolled a baby-shit green bike, with two flat tires, into the lobby of our building and said to me, "I found it unchained outside, you want it?". I say again, God is timing.

The rest is history. I walked the bike up to 96th Street, where the next morning I got it repaired and given two new tires. Everything else on the bike was vintage 1971, a year older than me. A book rack behind the seat, a leather Brooks saddle, original grips, and three speeds: going up, riding flat and going down.

Unlike many other bikes of her kind, she bears her name only on the chain guard. A Raleigh Superbe. Pronounced in England with a snotty accent, "superb", but in Manhattan her name is obviously Superbe, pronounced "Super Be", with a hard "e". Better than Superman, I implore her every time we ride to, "Fly SuperBe! Flllyyyyy!!"

When I ride, I am flirting with the world, sitting as tall and straight as the Empire State.

Why is it that people say, "It's just like riding a bike, once you've done it, you never forget how."? There's a truth to the fact that if you've ever peddled a bicycle, you can do it again. It has something to do with everyone's inherent child. We're all angels whether we hide our wings or not. O you women, and men, you old and young once you give over to two wheels, the only damage that you may suffer will be to your pant legs. And the rewards are free.

Biking may not make you any money, but you will save plenty. You'll save at least a thousand bucks a year that other people give the MTA for the privilege of catapulting themselves in underground death traps. The only thing that keeps a bike rider from a prompt schedule is a flat tire, and even if that occurs, you're still not trapped below.

If you have a bike in Manhattan, you will be able to fly. It's that easy. This book should be re-titled to, "My Life as An Idiot" or "How to Live in A Police State (and still feel free)".

Some people can adjust their spines up against the trunks of trees, and there are some who can align themselves to a perfectly straight sidewalk as they walk down the street. For those who ride two wheels, constantly moving forward, there is a defiance of gravity, a balance that hooks a rider to an acute awareness of everything. It's the most active Zen I can think of. It's my kind: "I want to be Zen!" So, my meditation, as it were, my yoga, happens during my acts of self-transportation, getting myself from one place to the next.

Even though the city has gone through so many horrible changes in the past seven years, as it has gone through The Great Sanitation of the Giuliani regime, one thing did not change. Traffic. I doubt, as bad as it may get, that Manhattan's traffic lights will ever go dark. Though, if that glorious day of freedom on this island were to occur, bicyclists wouldn't have a problem, they bike without regard for the reds anyway.

Garbage trucks are the whales that feed almost exclusively at night. Nothing can get in the way of their feast, if they're blocking car traffic, the cars have to wait. Fortunately, not even a whale can stop a minnow on two wheels.

When they scream, "Get a car," scream back, "Get a life!"

Get Out of Egypt

A new Passover classic. Played with tenor banjo.

Sometimes it feels like we're slaves in secret
All work and no play, should we get out of Egypt?
We can't live anymore on the straight and narrow
Could we open the door and say, "No more," to Pharaoh?

Get out, get out, get out, get out
No more, no more, no more, no more Say, "No more," to Pharaoh and
Get out of Egypt

How can we act while riddled with fear?
Where's truth? What's fact? O get fear out of here
In myself and my kin this freedom seed's been planted
Grab hands and begin just take no more for granted

Get out, get out, get out, get out
No more, no more, no more, no more Take no more for granted
Get fear out of here
Say, "No more," to Pharaoh and "Get out of Egypt."

Pharaoh's only rule is to stay in his tower
Use the People like tools till we find our own power
We want Life to have less stress and violence
We'll be on our way when there's no more silence

Get out, get out, get out, get out
No more, no more, no more, no more
No more silence
Find our own power
Take no more for granted

Get fear out of here
"No more," to Pharaoh and, "Get out of Egypt"

Rebellion whispers through the years, do you hear it?
"Love's more precious than gold go invest our spirit
There's enough to share, we have what we need
Kindness and care, not corporate greed

Get out, get out, get out, get out
No more, no more, no more, no more
No corporate greed
Invest our spirit
No more silence
Find our own power
Take no more for granted
Get fear out of here
Say, "No more," to Pharaoh and
"Get out of Egypt"

How's about a future with peace and respect?
Sharin' joy with Mother Earth and the Universe that's perfect
We can't take any more of the Pharoah's slave order
After seven thousand years, how 'bout no more borders?

Get out, get out, get out, get out
No more, no more, no more, no more
Say no more borders
The Universe is perfect
No corporate greed
Invest our spirit
No more silence
Find our own power
Take no more for granted
Get fear out of here
Say, "No more," to Pharaoh x2
and Get out of Egypt
Get out of Egypt we got to go on and GET OUT OF EGYPT

THE COLOR SONGS

Songs written while wandering Europe. The first began from a balcony in Paris on a grey morning, seeing a yellow shop. Sung acapella. Made for animation.

Yellow

I want a yellow life
And a yellow wife
Who'll cut me lemon meringue pie
With a yellow knife

I want a yellow car
That goes beep beep beep
I want a yellow house
On a yellow street

So people will call me the fellow
Who is mellow
And they will say that mellow fellow is, you know
He is yellow

I want a yellow shop
That sells banana pies
I want a yellow dog
With yellow eyes
    Woof! Shh. *Woof!*
Shhh Come here. Sit down. Good dog.

I want a yellow world
Around a yellow sun
So all us yellow people
Can have some yellow fun

And I will be happy
Eatin' yellow snackies
And I know it sounds sappy
But there's one, one darn thing in this world that I want
And that's to BELLOW, that I'm yellow
A mellow fellow
I'm beautiful sunshine yellow.

64

Red

The tomato sauce is red-a
The pepperoni is red-a
I must be out of my head-a
My whole pizza pie is red-a

The strawberry ice cream is red-a
The maraschino cherry's red-a
I must be out of my head-a
My whole sundae looks-a like-a red-a

I love to smell the red-a rose
Smelling the perfume in my red-a nose
And so the story goes
I like to dance without my red-a clothes

I love everything that's red-a
I must be outta my head-a
I love everything that's red-a
I must be outta my head-a

Orange

Orange you glad you're orange (doo wah ahh)
Orange you glad you're not grey, hey hey
Orange you glad you're round (like a ball)
Orange you glad you're not square, not at all

Orange you sweet, orange you neat
Orange you be, be, be, bah, do, wah, do, wah'n

All the way from Florida (doo wah ahh)
Where there is more of ya (doo wah ahh)

You're the tops, you're the juice in my cup
You're le grande, you're the leader of a big brass band
You're the one, that ripens under the sun
You're the most important, cause you're orange
You're neat, you're sweet, you kick me off of my feet
You're orange
Bah, do ,wah, do, wah, do, wah
Bah, do, do, bah, do, do, wah
You're orange

Moses in Five Acts

a play to share for Passover

by Rebbe Wally

CHARACTERS
Pharaoh
Storyteller(s)
The Mother
Baby
Miriam
Princess
Moses
Aaron
Slave Masters
Slaves
Former Slave

PROPS
The Pharaoh's announcement sign
A basket for the baby
Scallions for whips
A rug or fabric for The Red Sea

NOTE: Music playlist available on Spotify.

PROLOGUE
Pharaoh puts up a sign that reads: "PHARAOH'S LAW: Death to your first-born son. Starting now."

ACT ONE – A MOTHER'S COURAGE

Storyteller: Many, many moons ago, a mother sends her baby boy down the river in order to save him because she was caught between life and the Pharaoh's law. She builds him a small ark and sends him to an uncertain future.

(Participants slowly pass around a basket with the smallest child or doll in it while whispering words of encouragement or making sounds of a river. And/or you can sing "Swing Low" with Hank Williams.)

Chorus: Swing low, sweet chariot
Coming for to carry me home,
Swing low, sweet chariot,
Coming for to carry me home.
I looked over Egypt, and what did I see
Coming for to carry me home?
A band of angels coming after me,
Coming for to carry me home.

Repeat chorus.

(The **Mother** weeps by the riverside then makes a solemn wish.)

Mother: Oh river, carry my son safely so he may grow in a land that is free.

ACT TWO – PHARAOH'S DAUGHTER

(**Princess**, the Pharaoh's daughter, goes to the river and swims.)

Storyteller: The next morning, miles and miles away, Princess, the Pharaoh's daughter, was swimming in a river with her friend Miriam who was from a different class and race. Together they transcend the boundaries of society, envisioning something new. As the sun starts to sparkle on the water the two friends see something floating peacefully down the river.

Miriam: Hello duck.

Princess: Hello baby.

Miriam: You're as calm as the water.

Princess: We'll name you Moses. You are welcome into our life Moses.

Miriam: Thanks for coming.

(**Moses** enters.)

Storyteller: Miriam and the Princess raise Moses so he would know the truth of his relationship with the river that delivered him. Moses grows up in the flow.

Moses: I am in this world by the grace of three mothers, the mother who gave birth to me, the mother that fished me out of the river and Mother Nature herself.

ACT THREE - MOSES GROWS UP

Storyteller: Moses and his estranged older brother Aaron, a prophet too, grew up around slavery.

Song: Chain Gang by Sam Cooke.

(**Slaves** work and are repeatedly beaten by **Slave Masters** with scallions.)

Slave Masters: *(repeated)* Keep working! Keep working!!

Slaves: *(repeated)* Oy! Oy!! Oy! Oy!!

Storyteller: One day Moses murdered a Slave Master who was hurting a worker badly.

(Moses murders a Slave Master.)

Moses: Oh no, what a mistake! I should be non-violent at all times. Peace can only come after empathy.

ACT FOUR – GETTING THROUGH TO PHARAOH

(Aaron and Moses go to see Pharaoh.)

Storyteller: Moses and his brother Aaron go to Pharaoh and try to persuade him to let the slaves be free.

Aaron: Be reasonable Pharaoh.

Moses: Be kind.

Pharaoh: No!

Aaron: Come on!

Moses: Let my people go!

Pharaoh: I said, No.

Storyteller: Because Pharaoh doesn't budge the Universe conspires to assist with Moses' one big wish. Ten plagues visit Egypt.

Song: Axioms by Ken Butler.

ALL: To sacrifice some of our pleasure in honor of the real plagues of our Earth, lets take out a drop of wine from our cup for each plague.
Everyone around the table places ten drops of wine on their plates as they say the Ten Plagues. The ensemble should act out each of the plagues.
1. Pollution and privatization of water / Blood; 2. Frogs dead and maimed by chemicals; 3. Poverty / Lice; 4. extinction of thousands of species / Swarms; 5. mad cow disease/ Pestilence; 6. collapse of health care / Boils; 7. radical climate change / Hail; 8. famine & genetically modified foods / Locusts; 9. Darkness; 10. War & violence / death of the Egyptian first born.

Storyteller: Only after every Egyptian's first-born son dies does Pharaoh change his mind.

Moses: How about now?

Pharaoh: Get out of here!

ACT FIVE – EXODUS

Storyteller: The Pharaoh's bullies and thugs harassed and tortured the slaves as they left. They pursued them all the way to the Red Sea.

(Moses, Aaron, Miriam and the Slaves come to the Red Sea.)

Aaron: *(to Moses)* Now what are we going to do?

Miriam: *(to everyone)* What can we do now?!

Slaves: We can't go back.

Moses: *(inspired)* Fear not friends, look forward. In your thoughts say to the sea, "The sea is receding, thank you for doing that." Repeat it.

Everyone: *(repeat quietly)* The sea is receding, thank you for doing that.

Aaron: The water is going down, let's go everyone!

Storyteller: As soon as they were safe the red sea swelled again washing all the Pharaoh's soldiers away. Miriam led the women and the rest in a joyful celebration.

Song: Bob Marley's "Exodus". Big dance break.

(Pour **Miriam's Cup**, a cup of water because waters birth new possibility. Refill water glasses.)

Storyteller: Miriam led the women in rejoicing as the Red Sea waters broke and made their escape final. In the desert Miriam called forth the well of water that nourished the runaway slaves. In honor of Miriam, we enjoy our water.

EPILOGUE

Storyteller: Over a million people wandered around the desert for a very long time.

Former Slave: We put the Oy back in unemployment.

Storyteller: During their psychedelic journey Moses spoke to a burning bush, he talked with spirits on top of a mountain, and he came down from that mountain with Ten Commandments that everyone is supposed to live by.

Moses: *To All.* Do you know the commandments? How many do we live by? Why do they matter?

(Listen to response.)

Storyteller: Thanks for retelling the story of the exodus from Egypt. Welcome back to our present day. Now onward.

(Applause. Bows.)

Song: Oddisee's "That's Love".

The Tale of the Thanksgiving Ladybug

By Wally

Dedicated to the children of Mother Earth with gratitude and love.

Dinner theatre for 4 – 16 people to play.

CHARACTERS

Host 1 & 2

Storyteller 1, 2 & 3

Ladybug

Earth

Sun

Plant

Tree

Animal

Human Being

Wind

Birds

Rain / Water

Moon

NOTE: Music playlist available on Spotify.

(MUSIC: Pre-show song "Thanks for Calling' By Chris Rael.

All lights are turned off. HOST rings a bell as HOST2 lights a candle.)

HOST: We are thankful for so much because before this, there was only darkness.

HOST2: *(with candle)* Thanksgiving: a word that best describes the simultaneous nature of giving and taking, just like stars and this candle they give light as it consumes energy. Thanksgiving.

(MUSIC: "Gratitude" by Earth, Wind & Fire.)

HOST: Now let's feast on <u>The Tale of the Thanksgiving Ladybug</u>!

HOST 2: Please welcome the Ladybug with a round of applause.

(STORYTELLERS enter with LADYBUG who sits in an empty space.)

STORYTELLER: Once upon a time there was a ladybug that was born into darkness, like a speck of red on a black velvet elephant.

LADYBUG: *(afraid)* Where am I? Who am I? What's going on?!

(MUSIC: "In This Temple …" by Sufjan Stevens.)

STORYTELLER2: She remained like this until something changed.

STORYTELLER3: Her tiny foot landed on something.

STORYTELLER: And a voice spoke from within.

EARTH: Ladybug, ladybug, I am your Earth Mother. I care for you continuously and abundantly throughout time. I have gemstones and crystals to keep you healthy and vibrant, to bring you into balance and harmony with all.

STORYTELLER2: For Mother Earth, the ladybug was very grateful.

LADYBUG: *(hugging Earth)* Thank you so much.

STORYTELLER3: But it was dark around her and she felt lonely.

STORYTELLER: Until one morning, after a long night's dream, the sun appeared.

(MUSIC: "Here Comes the Sun", Nina Simone's cover.)

LADYBUG: Hello.

SUN: Ladybug, ladybug, I am your older brother the Sun. Each day I bring the light, the energy source of all life on Earth. I shine, you shine and we all shine.

STORYTELLER2: For the Sun, the ladybug was quite thankful.

LADYBUG: Thank you!

STORYTELLER3: Now that the ladybug can see the world around her she realizes that she is on top of a green plant.

(MUSIC: "Atoms for Peace" groove, Thom Yorke.)

LADYBUG: Oh hello!

PLANT: Ladybug, ladybug, I am one of many kinds of plants and flowers that live upon the Earth, to beautify and sustain her. We breathe together.

LADYBUG: Yes we do. *(breath)* Merci.

STORYTELLER: For the plants and flowers, the ladybug jumped for joy!

STORYTELLER2: *(as LADYBUG jumps)* Boing, boing, BOING!

STORYTELLER3: *(the LADYBUG flies)* And she landed on a tree.

71

(MUSIC: *More Today Than Yesterday* by The Spiral Staircase.)

LADYBUG: *(to Tree)* Hello tree.

TREES: Ladybug, ladybug, we Trees give you shelter, food and paper products. We grab hold of the soil below us while reaching to the sky. We are a reminder that everything expands and grows in all directions.

STORYTELLER: For trees, the ladybug was deeply grateful.

LADYBUG: Thanks Trees!

STORYTELLER2: And as she sat on a leaf, she saw below her many, many different animals.

(MUSIC: "The Lion Sleeps Tonight" by Ladysmith Black Mambazo.)

*Everyone makes **animals with sounds**. **Bold** letters denote unison fun.)*

LADYBUG: Woof! Meow? Hello!

ANIMALS: Ladybug, ladybug, the Animals are here to teach the Humans. Each different animal has a piece of wisdom of how to live this life. The dog teaches us devotion and love. The rat shows us how to survive. The cat reminds us to purr when we feel good.

STORYTELLER3: For all the animals, the ladybug was happily thankful.

LADYBUG: You are so wonderful, gracias!!!

STORYTELLER: Then one day, amongst the animals, the ladybug saw human beings walking around.

(MUSIC: "People" by the Supremes. **"peas and carrots ..."**)

HUMAN BEING: Ladybug, ladybug we People bring words, thoughts and feelings to our journey, which assists us in finding our way.

STORYTELLER2: The ladybug was very grateful for humans.

LADYBUG: You're great!

STORYTELLER3: Then a wind blew, carrying our ladybug into the air.

(MUSIC: "The Wind" by Cat Stevens. **Wind**.)

WIND: Ladybug, ladybug we are the four winds who continue to blow and cleanse the air. With wind, our minds are cleared and our ships set sail.

STORYTELLER: The ladybug loved the wind.

LADYBUG: Thank you north, south, east and west winds.

STORYTELLER2: While flying around she saw lots of birds in the air.

(MUSIC: "Interlude" by Tribal Baroque with Waterstrider. **Tweet tweet**.)

BIRDS: Ladybug, ladybug we are the birds. We find a place to live in the world and sing the song of that place so that our spirits might be lifted by sweet sound.

STORYTELLER3: The ladybug was thankful for birds and their songs.

LADYBUG: Tweet, tweet!

STORYTELLER: And, all of a sudden it started to rain.

(MUSIC: *"Alanson, Crooked River" by Sufjan Stevens*. **Make rain**.)

RAIN / WATER: Ladybug, ladybug we are the Waters of the Earth, here to quench thirst and to help keep us clean. We flow in water.

LADYBUG: Thank you water.

STORYTELLER2: The ladybug was really thankful for rain and water.

STORYTELLER3: While looking into the rivers, lakes and oceans, she saw many colorful creatures.

LADYBUG: Hi fish.

(MUSIC: *"Sea Ocean Waves" plays*. **Move like fish**.)

FISH: Ladybug, ladybug we are the beings, seen and unseen, that thrive in the water. We sustain villages and remind all to keep moving with ease.

STORYTELLER: The ladybug was grateful for all the water beings.

LADYBUG: Thanks for flowing fish.

STORYTELLER2: Then in the reflection of the calm water, the ladybug saw the Moon and the Moon saw the ladybug.

LADYBUG: Hi, Moon.

(MUSIC: *"What A Little Moonlight Can Do" by Billie Holiday*.)

MOON: Ladybug, ladybug I am your grandmother, the Moon. I hold hands with all the women of the world and bind them together with the rhythms of the Waters, reflecting light into the darkness.

LADYBUG: I'm so very grateful.

STORYTELLER3: And everyone felt so grateful they sang in unison.

(MUSIC: *"Grateful" by Hezekiah Walker*. Start at 3:15.

Everyone lip-syncs, *getting more deeply felt with each refrain*.)

EVERYONE: Grateful, grateful, grateful, grateful *(x2)*

Grateful, grateful, grateful, gratefulness is flowing from my heart. *(all x3)*

73

LADYBUG: Thank you everyone! There is no need to fear anything! We have and we are all that we need. Thank you. Oh, thank you.

(Everything shifts to profound silence and listening.)

STORYTELLER: The ladybug stared at the Moon, grateful for her Grandmother.

STORYTELLER2: And as she sat still and quiet in a very special place, she felt the great flowing Spirit, the unnamable …

STORYTELLER3: Wa, wa, wa, wa, wa, wa, wa, wa, wa, wa, wa …

HOST: *(to everyone)* If you are feeling grateful for the energy that flows through you and all living things, please join together in a group WaWa. *(with everyone)* … wa, wa, wa, wa, wa, wa, wa, wa, wa, …

EVERYONE: Wa, wa, wa, wa, wa, wa, wa, wa, wa, wa … *(ad infinitum)*

HOST 2: *(after awhile)* Let us know peace.

EVERYONE: Yes. For as long as the moon shall rise,

for as long as the rivers shall flow,

for as long as the sun shines,

for as long as the grass grows, let us know peace.

STORYTELLERS: And then all of us, will live happily ever after.

(MUSIC: "Gratitude" by Earth, Wind & Fire.

Everyone dances.)

THE END

(l to r) Ruby Sunrise, Lucy Blum, Gregory Linington, and Jonah Cooper in his debut performance as the Ladybug.

INTRODUCING:
The Breasts of Tiresias: A Surrealist Musical

My longest relationship in the theatre is with Guillaume Apollinaire's "surrealist drama" *Les mamelles de Tirésias*. I was cast as The Husband in a production of Louis Simpson's translation, paired with Eugene Ionesco's *The Bald Soprano*. The Simpson translation highlighted an abstraction of reason that was fun though incomprehensible, absurd for absurdity's sake, but Apollinaire's play inseminated me. I loved being pregnant and having children, like a man. When given the opportunity to direct something at the Knitting Factory's AlterKnit Theatre in 1996, my mom suggested that I consider *Breasts*. I listened and brought together poet Molly Findlay and composer Jeremy Bernstein to go back to the original text to see what heart and reason we could find.

Apollinaire's play was written before World War One and finished after the war adding only the Prologue where the Director addresses the audience. I cut passages from the speech that spoke to envisioning a new theatre where the action would surround and be within the audience. Both productions of *Breasts* have utilized every inch of the theatre for play.

I remember my tears as I read the Prologue to *Breasts* to my friend and producer Amy Wood in an Alphabet City vegetarian café. After serendipitous wonderment, involving a Parisian theatre producer, we collaborated on a Parisian production of *Breasts* with a French cast.

Just a year before the 2010 production a new *Breasts* translation by poet Maya Slater came out and further illuminated truths inside the poetry. Further, poet Rachel Kann was invited to contribute Tiresias' speech which we hear during the interval of the play proper. I added it in, along with The Ikettes' recording of "I'm Blue", Ray Charles and Betty Carter's recording of "Two to Tango", and Lou Reed's lyrics to "There Is No Time" for an encore.

In New York City, the *Village Voice* called it "forty-five manic minutes of amazing theatre." In Paris *Froggie's Delight* wrote, "Fidelity and modernity, an excess of expression and the precision of the text, dream and reality, past and present, this production is a veritable experience in its entirety."

The Breasts of Tirésias
A Surrealist Musical

(based on Guillaume Apollinaire's *Les Mamelles de Tirésias*)

Adapted and directed by

Eric "Wally" Wallach

Music by

Madeleine Besson and Jeremy Bernstein

AMY WOOD, Producer

presents

The Breasts of Tiresias

A Surrealist Musical

(based on **Guillaume Apollinaire's** *Les Mamelles de Tirésias*)

Adapted and Directed by
ERIC "WALLY" WALLACH

Music by
JEREMY BERNSTEIN and **MADELEINE BESSON**

Starring
Madeleine Besson as The People of Zanzibar
Astrid Bayiha as Therese / Tiresias
ThomaS Landbo as The Husband
Emilie Chevrillon as The Policeman
Sebastien Vion as Presto / The Son
Thomas Dalle as Lacouf / The Journalist

Virginie Fremont / Sara Renaud … Scene Design/Fabrication
Severine Fremont … Costume Design
Ruddy Fritsch … Light Design
Jeremy Bernstein … Sound Design
Hillary Andular … Video Design
Diana Fontannaz … Asst. Director, Dialect Coach and S.M.
Amy Wood … Associate Director

PRODUCED IN COLLABORATION WITH
THÉÂTRE DE LA REINE BLANCHE
DEBUTED ON AUGUST 26, 2010

CHARACTERS

THE DIRECTOR

THERESE / TIRESIAS

THE HUSBAND

THE POLICEMAN

PRESTO

LACOUF

REPORTER #1

REPORTER #2

THE PEOPLE OF ZANZIBAR

THE JOURNALIST

THE SON

A LADY IN THE AUDIENCE

TIME: Now
PLACE: Zanzibar

All lines **in bold** are sung.

Please Note:

Text has been used by translator/poets Louis Simpson (1960), Maya Slater (2009), Molly Findlay (1996), along with poet Rachel Kann who wrote Tiresias' speech in the interval. Lou Reed is quoted and more for the encore. Also, the cover photo is by Alejandro Guerrero.

LOVE or DIE

PRE-SHOW

(As the public enters Zanzibar, they hear music from local radio stations. **The People of Zanzibar** *enters to the piano and the public.)*

People of Zanzibar

Welcome to Zanzibar.

*(***The People of Zanzibar** *plays at the piano.* **Presto** *is playing a gambling dice game with the public.* **The Policeman** *maintains order.* **Lacouf** *mingles about.* **Presto** *and* **Lacouf** *introduce* **The People of Zanzibar** *with applause then close the curtain and introduce* **The Director** *who comes to the stage with a candle and lights it.)*

PROLOGUE

Director

So here I am back among you

Back with a dynamic company

I'm back on the stage

But sadly, I've found

The theatre without greatness or virtue

A theatre that kills only the time

And shows the sin but does not show the savior

But the hour has struck the hour of humanity

Right now

All of us who have been living with war we hear it

I was in the army making war

On the northern front commanding troops

One night when in the sky the light from all the stars

Twinkled up above like eyes of new-born babies

All of a sudden, a thousand rockets rose from the opposite trenches

Rousing the guns of the enemy

I remember it as though it were yesterday

I could hear them go up but not come down

Then from the observation post there came

The message that the range of the enemy guns was so immense

The explosions could no longer be heard

And all the soldiers watching at their posts

Announced the stars were darkening one by one

Then the whole army started shouting

Director + someone else

THEY'RE PUTTING OUT THE STARS WITH GUNFIRE

Director

The stars were dying in the fine autumn sky

We were dying there of the death of stars

And on that murky front with its gray light

We could only say in despair

Director + someone else

THEY'VE EVEN MURDERED THE CONSTELLATIONS

Director

But in a great voice out of a speaker

From some sort of supreme headquarters

The voice of the unknown captain who always saves us cried

    THE TIME HAS COME TO LIGHT THE STARS AGAIN

And the whole army let it out

All

FIRE AT WILL

Director

The gunners hastened

The marksmen fired

And the sublime stars lit up again one by one

Our shells rekindled their eternal fire

The enemy guns fell silent, dazzled

By the scintillating of all the stars

Voila, there is the history of all the stars

And since that night I too light one by one

All the stars within that were extinguished

So here I am back with you

My company don't be impatient

Public ne soyez pas impatients

I bring you a musical that aims to reform society

It's about children in the family

And as it is a domestic subject

We're giving it a homely treatment

The actors will not put on a mean tone

They will simply appeal to your common sense

And above all they'll try to entertain you

So that you will be inclined to profit

From all the lessons that the play contains

And so that the earth will be starred with the glances of infants

More numerous than the twinkling stars

Public hear the lesson of war

Make children now you couples that thought you couldn't afford it

or the world was too dark

We're trying to bring a new spirit to the theatre

A joyfulness ecstasy virtue

And let us be clear now in this moment together

That the playwright director has the right

To create what they will without regard to the government's law

Or the laws of time and space

Forgive me my friends my company

Excusez-moi ladies and gentlemen

It's been so long since I have been with you

But out there there's still a spark

Where they're putting out the smoking stars

And those who light them again are asking, demanding you

To raise yourselves up to the height of those magnificent flames

And also burn

O friends

Be the unquenchable torch of the new fire

People of Zanzibar

O friends

Be the torch of the new fire

ACT 1, SCENE 1

*(The kettle whistles, the bell rings. Lights up on **Therese** at the stove.)*

Therese

No Mister husband

You won't make me do what you want

(Whisper) I am a woman and I don't recognize the authority of men

Besides I want to do things my way

Men have been doing what they want long enough

After all I too want to go and fight for freedom

I want to be a soldier hup two hup two

I want to make war *(Thunder)*

And not make children

No Mister husband you won't order me around anymore

Because you made love to me in Connecticut

Doesn't mean I have to cook for you in Zanzibar

Husband

Give me bacon I tell you give me bacon

Therese

Listen to him all he thinks about is sex

(She has a fit of hysterics)

But you haven't the faintest idea you schmuck

(Sneeze)

After being a soldier I want to be an artist

(Sneeze)

Absolutely absolutely

(Sneeze)

I also want to be a deputy a lawyer a senator

(Two sneezes)

A minister the president of the state

(Sneeze)

And I want to be a doctor curing bodies or brains

Pouncing around Europe and America as I please

Making babies cooking meals no it's too much

(She cackles)

I want to be a philosopher chemist mathematician

A waitress in a restaurant a savvy dietician

And then if I please I should quite like to keep

The tired old dancer whose talent runs deep

<u>Husband</u>

Give me bacon I tell you give me bacon

<u>Therese</u>

Listen to him all he thinks about is sex

(She has a bit of hysterics)

Eat your own pig's feet

But I think I'm sprouting a beard

My breasts are coming loose

(She utters a cry and opens her blouse from which her breasts emerge, one red, the other blue, and lets them rise, toy balloons attached by strings.)

Fly away birds of my frailty

Et cetera

How pretty are feminine charms

They're utterly delicious

Good enough to eat

But enough of this nonsense

85

Let's not go in for aeronautics

There is always some advantage in being virtuous

Vice is a dangerous business after all

That is why it is better to sacrifice beauty

That may be a cause of fornication

Let's get rid of my tits

(She pops the balloons.)

But it's not just my beard my mustache is growing too

Damn, I look like a wheatfield ripe for the harvest

I feel as virile as the devil

A stallion with scorn

From my head on down to my hooves

I'm a bull packing horns

I'll be a torero (x2)

But let's not go on

Spreading the news of my future O hero

Put up your dukes

And you my poor husband less virile than I

You can sound the alarm till the bell tower's dry

SCENE 2

<u>Husband</u>

I tell you I want some bacon

<u>Therese</u>

Eat your own pig's feet

86

(Therese cackles. He approaches as though to hit her.)

Husband

Oh but this isn't my wife Therese

Who is this lout who's wearing her clothes

No doubt he's a murderer and he has killed her

Therese where are you baby

But you, you vile rascal disguised as my Therese

I'm going to kill you

(They fight, she overpowers him.)

Therese

You're right I'm not your wife anymore

Husband

Oh really

Therese

And yet I am Therese

Husband

Oh really?

Therese

But Therese who is not a woman now

Husband

This is too much

87

Therese

So now that I've become a good-looking guy

Husband

Detail that I missed

Therese

From now on I'll have a man's name Tiresias

Husband

Adiosias

Adiosias Tiresias

Adios adios adios

Adiosias Tiresias

SCENE 3

Tiresias

I'm outta here

Husband

Adios

*(**Tiresias** lets in two movers who take everything. **Tiresias** and **The People of Zanzibar** trash the apartment then vacuum.)*

The piano

The violin

The butter dish this is getting serious

*(Earthquake. Alone, **The Husband** dances to "I'm Blue" by The Ikettes.)*

SCENE 4

*(**Presto** and **Lacouf** enter as **Tiresias** and **The People of Zanzibar** hurl themselves on **The Husband**. **Tiresias** takes off his trousers, undresses herself, hands him the skirt and puts on the trousers. **The People of Zanzibar** tie him up.)*

<u>Presto</u>

Lacouf, mon frère, I've lost at zanzi

All that I hope to you

<u>Lacouf</u>

Presto, mon frère, I've won nothing

Besides what has Zanzibar got to do with it you are in Paris

<u>Presto</u>

In Zanzibar

<u>Lacouf</u>

In Paris

<u>Presto</u>

This is too much

After ten years of friendship

And all the dreadful things I've always said about you

<u>Lacouf</u>

Too bad did I ever ask a favor of you, you're in Paris

<u>Presto</u>

In Zanzibar, the proof is I've lost everything

89

Lacouf

Mister Presto we'll have to fight

Presto

Yes, we must

Lacouf

On equal terms

Presto

As you please

In this life you never know what's going to hit you

*(They aim at each other. **The People of Zanzibar** fire two shots as they fall.)*

Tiresias

Beloved freedom I've won you at last

First, I'll check the news

To find out what's just happened

TF1 (on video)

As he lost in Zanzibar

Mister Presto has lost his bet

The whole exacta, for we're in Paris

*(**Presto** and **Lacouf** get up. **The People of Zanzibar** fire two shots, as the duelists fall down again.)*

France 2 (on video)

Mister Lacouf has won nothing

Since they played at Zanzibar

Just as this play is in Paris

(Presto and Lacouf get up, The People of Zanzibar fire two shots, the duelists fall down. Tiresias appears in the audience.)

Tiresias

Now the universe is mine

The women are mine   mine is the government

I'm going to make myself town councilor

Yeah yeah yeah

The People of Zanzibar

Now the universe is yours

The women are yours, yours is the government

She's going to make herself town councilor

Yeah yeah yeah

(They duet for as long as they like. A police siren is heard.)

Tiresias

But I hear a noise

Maybe I'd better go

(The Policeman enters on a moped and dismounts.)

The Policeman

Nobody move

(The Policeman disperses the two bodies and sees The Husband bound.)

SCENE 5

<u>Policeman</u>

It stinks of crime round here

<u>Husband</u>

Ah! At last we have a representative

Of Zanzibarian authority

I'll introduce myself

Hey Mister if you've got any business with me

Be kind enough to take

My army papers out of my left pocket

<u>Policeman</u>

What a pretty girl

Tell me pretty child

Who has been treating you so badly

<u>Husband</u>

He thinks I'm a girl

If it's engagement you're seeking

Then begin by untying me

<u>Policeman</u>

What a pretty

What a pretty

What a pretty girl …

*(The Policeman unties him. Bells toll as **Presto** and **Lacouf** revive.)*

SCENE 6

Presto

I'm getting tired of being dead

Imagine there are people

Who find it more honorable to be dead than alive

Lacouf

Now you can see you weren't in Zanzibar

Presto

Yet that's the place to live

But I'm disgusted at us for fighting a duel

There's no doubt that people view death

Much too favorably

Lacouf

What do you expect

Our opinion of mankind is much too high

In the shit of jewelers

Do you expect pearls and diamonds

Presto

Greater marvels have been seen

Lacouf

In short Mister Presto

We don't have luck with gambling

But now you can see quite clearly that you were in Paris

Presto

In Zanzibar

Lacouf

Take aim

Presto

Fire

*(**The People of Zanzibar** unloads a semi-automatic and they fall.)*

Policeman

You're under arrest

*(**Presto** and **Lacouf** run off. **The Husband** tries to call Therese but gets her outgoing message, "you've reached Tiresias, leave a message." Beep.)*

SCENE 7

Policeman

The local gangsters

Won't prevent me from saying that I find you as pleasant to touch

As a lovely ball of rubber

Bubblehead

But who cares if

She's a pretty girl

Husband

You know, he's right

Since my wife is a man

It's fair that I be a woman

  (To the Policeman)

I am a decent woman-sir

My wife is a man-lady

She's taken the piano the violin and the butter dish

She's a soldier a minister mover of chests

Policeman

A chest nut

Husband

Nutty chester

Policeman

Chesty Lester

Husband

No she's chaste

Policeman

Chased with haste onto a train

Husband

In the rain

She's the conductor

Policeman

She can doctor

After all it's the art of healing people

Listen

(Parade music is heard.)

Husband

At the end of the day it's a matter of curing people

Music will do it

As well as any other cure

Policeman

That's fine

(The Policeman jumps on Husband and tries to take his dress off.)

Husband

Hey get off my back

Policeman

No resisting

Husband

I refuse to continue this conversation

Where is my wife

Voices of Soldiers

Long live Tiresias

No more babies no more babies

Long live Tiresias

No more babies no more babies

(The Policeman forces The People of Zanzibar to the keys.)

Policeman

Hey my sweet poppet slink roll up to the bar

I'll spin you a tune as you roll your cigar

'Bout the wife of the baker of Zanzibar

Who each seventh year has stolen the car

She sheds her skin by the light of a star

Husband

Hey my sweet poppet slink roll up to the bar

I'll spin you a tune as you roll your cigar

'Bout the wife of the baker of Zanzibar

Who each seventh year has stolen the car

She sheds her skin by the light of a star *(Policeman + Husband)*

All

She carries a joke too far (x3)

Policeman

Miss or Mrs. I'm crazy with love

For you

And I want to marry you I do

Husband

But don't you see that I'm a man

Policeman

Makes no difference I could PACS you

Husband

Nonsense

You'd do better having children

Policeman

Oh really

Voices of the Soldiers

Long live Tiresias

Long live long live General Tiresias

Long live long live Deputy Tiresias

No more babies no more babies

No more children no more children.

*(The **Husband** wanders in a storm, animals are howling in distress.)*

SCENE 8

Husband

Great representatives of high authority

You hear it it's been said clearly

Women at Zanzibar want their rights

And suddenly renounce reproductive nights

No more babies no more children you hear them shout

To fill Zanzibar there are elephants about

Monkeys and snakes mosquitoes and ostriches

But bees at least make wax and bring in the honey

Woman is only a neuter in heaven's eye

And you can take my word for that Mister policeman

Zanzibar needs children (x3)

Go and yell on the street corners on the boulevards

We must make children now in Zanzibar

Women won't have them too bad let men do it

Yes really and I mean to get right down to it

I'm not pretending

Policeman and Reporter #1

You

Reporter #2

You that shed tears at the play
Wish for children that conquer
Observe the measureless ardor
Born of the changing of sex

Husband

I will have offspring though I have no wife
To see how it is done come back to me tonight

Reporter #2 *(exiting)*

She's spinning a yarn
Which must be heard further than Zanzibar

Policeman

You will have offspring though you have no wife
To see how it is done I will come back tonight
To keep me waiting would be absurd
I will return I take you at your word

Reporter #1

The strip club and the bar
For this cop holds more charm
Than repeopling Zanzibar

SCENE 9

Presto enters, tickles Husband

How can we give such beings a name

Though physically she's just the same

To call her man's not playing the game

Policeman

I shall return this very night to see how nature can

Provide you with progeny without a woman

Husband

Well then return this night and see how nature can

Provide me with progeny without a woman

Policeman and Husband

I shall return this very night to see how nature can

Provide you with progeny without a woman

People of Zanzibar

Hey my sweet poppet slink roll up to the bar

I'll spin you a tune as you roll your cigar

'Bout the wife of the baker of Zanzibar

Who each seventh year has stolen the car

She sheds her skin by the light of a star

This gal she carries a joke too far…

*(The **ensemble** sings and dances together. Big finish.)*

100

All
Hey my sweet poppet slink roll up to the bar

I'll spin you a tune as you roll your cigar

'Bout the wife of the baker of Zanzibar

Who each seventh year has stolen the car

She sheds her skin by the light of a star (2x)

She carries a joke too far … (4x)   (*Curtain closes. End of act one.*)

INTERVAL

(**The People of Zanzibar** *sings deep waters and sister brother.* **Presto** *and* **Lacouf** *join for a boogie.* **The Policeman** *rids* **The People of Zanzibar** *from the piano with his gun.*)

People of Zanzibar
Hey, what did I do? Watch it. I didn't do nothing wrong. Do you see this?! I don't know why you're pointing a gun at me Mr. Policeman. Okay, I'm moving but under protest. I am being moved from the piano for no good reason! Okay, I'm going, but it's not right.

(**The Policeman** *sings dream a little dream with assistance from* **Presto** *and* **Lacouf**. *Curtain closes.* **General Tiresias** *addresses the audience.*)

General Tiresias
Ladies and ladies, your intention, please!

Hear me out, if need be, lock your knees

together!

However,

whether you are the camel type, and can hold on to one hump for many

moons, or are the type who needs more sugar, you can facilitate this revolution.

There is but one solution.

I am not on some Lysistrata type shit here, unless that is your fancy.

At the very least, arm yourselves with condoms, ladies!

We cannot make babies any longer.

The tick tock of a biological clock… it's a construct built by the literal DICKHEADS

Who got us in this mess in the first place.

Be a credit to your race. You were born to be more than a baby factory,

As a matter of fact that is actually the worst thing you can do with this wonder of a body.

No more shitting out bobble-headed rugrats distracting you from

the REAL work that must be done.

Grab your rubbers, grab your guns, let no more jizz up in your peachpit,

keep it pristine and sperm free! Think clearly!

These men, shooting off their dicks, they should tell us what to do?

Look at the mess that procreation has gotten us into.

Patriarchy is a pathetic evil.

Help save this nation from overpopulation and starvation.

No more miracles of birth unless what you are miraculously birthing is a brand new,

badass, motherfucking, YOU!

*(**Lacouf** and **Presto** play music and sing a Zanzibarien song. **The Husband** then crawls through the audience having violent contractions.)*

ACT 2, SCENE 1

*(**Babies** cry. The curtain opens revealing **The Husband**, trapped inside a large maternity dress.)*

<u>Husband</u>

Ah! The joys of fatherhood are simply wild

40,049 infants in one day alone

My happiness is complete

 (The babies get louder.)

Quiet quiet

Domestic bliss

No woman on my hands

 (The babies get louder.)

Shut up

Modern music is amazing

Nearly as amazing as the stage sets of those designers

Who flourish far from the Barbarians

At Zanzibar

You don't have to go to the Paris Theatre or the Russian Ballet

 (The babies get louder.)

Shut up

(One baby continues to cry.)

The time's come to swat 'em with belts on the bottom

Though it's discipline they need

I'd best be slow about it

I'll get them bicycles instead

And all these virtuosi

With talent to spare

Will give concer'

In the open air

(The babies quiet. He claps.)

Bravo bravo bravo

(Three knocks.)

Come in

SCENE 2

*(The **Journalist** enters.)*

Journalist

Hands up

Hullo Mister Husband Sir

I'm a Journalist from a Paris paper

Husband

From Paris

Make yourself at home

Journalist

The papers of Paris

a town in America

Hurrah

*(The **Journalist** unfolds a small American flag.)*

Have announced that you've discovered

The way for men

To make children

*(**The Journalist** blows his nose in the flag and puts it in his pocket.)*

Husband

That's the truth

Journalist

And how's it done

Husband

Willpower sir can achieve anything

Journalist

Are they colored or like normal people

Husband

It all depends on how you look at it

Journalist (dancing around)

You're wealthy I suppose

Husband

Not at all

Journalist

How will you bring them up?

Husband

After they've been bottle fed

I hope that they'll feed me instead

Journalist

In short you are something of a daughter-father

A maternalized paternal instinct; I guess

***(The Journalist** takes pictures of **The Husband**.)*

Husband

Au contraire Sir, it's all pure selfishness

Children are the wealth of the family

They're worth more than cash and a legacy

See that little sucker asleep in his cradle

(**Arthur** cries and drinks milk out of a biberon.)

His first name is Arthur and already he's made

A fortune with exclusive rights in curdled milk

(**Arthur** spits up milk.)

Journalist

He's advanced for his age

Husband

Joseph over here

(**Joseph** begins to cry.)

He's a novelist

His last novel sold 600,000 copies

Allow me to present you with one

Read at your leisure

(The **Journalist** lies down.)

Journalist

A lady whose name was Crapp

(He laughs on the four vowel sounds: a, e, i, o, a, e, i, o ...)

Husband

Nevertheless there is a refinement of expression here

Journalist

Ha! Ha! ah! ah!

Husband

A certain precociousness

Journalist

Hee! eh!

Husband

Which is way out of the ordinary

Journalist

Hands up

Husband

Now just as it stands

The novel has put into my hands

Almost two hundred thousand yen

Plus a literary prize

Consisting of twenty cases of dynamite

Journalist (exiting downstage)

Good-bye

Husband

Don't be afraid they're in my safety deposit vault at the bank

Journalist

All right

Don't you have any daughters

Husband

Sure I do this one she's divorced

(She cries.)

From the potato king

Gets a hundred thousand dollars alimony

*(The **Baby**, in a beret, cries, mumbling nonsense.)*

And this one the most creative artist in Zanzibar

She recites lovely verses on dull evenings

Her fire and genius earn as much

As a poet earns in fifty thousand years

Journalist

Congratulations my dear chap

But you've got some dust

On your dust coat

*(The **Journalist** picks up the speck of dust off of the husband.)*

Since you're so rich lend me a hundred bucks

Husband

Put that dust back

*(The **children** cry. **The Husband** shoots at the **Journalist**. **Children** exit.)*

SCENE 3

Husband

Well yes it's as simple as a periscope

The more children I have

The richer I'll be and the better I'll live

They say the codfish lays enough eggs in a day

To feed the entire world for a whole year

With fish soup and garlic

Isn't it wonderful to have a big family

Who are those idiotic economists

Who've made us believe that children

Spell poverty

When it's just the opposite

Did you ever hear of a cod starving to death

That's why I'll go on having children

First let's make a journalist

So I'll know everything

I'll predict the extras

And invent the rest

He must be capable of every chore

And able to write for every party

What a fine Journalist he'll be

Factual reports in-depth articles

Et cetera

He needs a blood supply from ink cartridges

He needs a spine

Some brains for not thinking with

A tongue - all the better for driveling

Lastly, he's got to have a song to sing

Come on kid, sing

(*Thunder and lighting. The form of the disfigured* **Son** *is in the audience.*)

109

SCENE 4

*(**The Husband** repeats "one, two." Till the end of the song.)*

<u>Son</u>

Dear daddy

If you want a closer look

At the activities of every crook

You've got to let me have some pocket money

Dear daddy

The tree of print is leafy

Every bough flaps like a banner

The fruit hangs in bunches

Papers have grown you ought to pick them now

And make the little kiddies salad lunches

Dear daddy

If you let me have five hundred bucks

I won't tell what I know about you

If you don't I'll tell them that your pretty young

Wife has a thousand babies baking in the oven

Dear daddy

I'll compromise you and I'll tell them that you've

Stolen and killed and had your way with the children

<u>Husband</u>

Bravo there's a vocalist

<u>Son</u>

Dear parents in one man

If you want to know last night's news

Here goes

A great blaze destroyed half of Baghdad

110

Husband

Too bad

Son

Mr. Eugene McKween of Central Cement Incorporation
Swallowed some juice
And got him a noose
Well that's what sources say from Investigation

Husband

Is he my relation

Son

The princess of Wales they say
Is marrying a girl today
Simply a meeting on the subway

Husband

What's it to me do I know those people
I want to hear good news about my friends

Son

We hear praise from New York
That Virginie Fremont's new work
Can charm like a dandy
As sweet as your candy

Husband

Long live the hammer of Fremont
O my son

Until next time I know right now

All that I need to know

About yesterday

Son

I'm going off to invent what's happening tomorrow

Husband

Bon voyage

SCENE 5

Husband (con't)

That one's good for nothing

I've a good mind to cut him out of my will

*(Three **Papparazzis** enter the home through the window with cameras.)*

Enough! Enough! I say

What a dumb idea to make the Press my friend

They just won't go away

They'll bother me all day

It has damn well got to end

*(The **Papparazzis** circle the **Husband**.)*

Hullo hullo Miss

I don't want your telephone service

I'm de-subscribing

112

*(The **Papparazzis** exit. The **Husband** comes out of the dress and gets rid of it.)*

Change of plan

No more useless mouths to feed

I need to cut down economize

First of all I'll make a tailor-child

Then I could be well dressed for a little walk

And as I'm not so bad to look at

Attract pretty people time and time again

SCENE 6

*(The **Policeman** with hair down and an exotic flower.)*

Policeman

Fine things you've been up to

You've kept your word

40,050 children in one day

You're rocking the boat

Husband

I'm coining it in

Policeman

But the people of Zanzibar

Famished by this excess of mouths to feed

Will soon be dying of hunger

Husband

Let them eat credit cards that makes up for everything

Policeman
Where do we get them?

Husband
From the Tarot reader

Policeman
From the Fortuneteller

Husband
Sacre Bleu! Cause we're thinking of the future

SCENE 7

Fortuneteller *(entering)*
Chaste citizens of Zanzibar I am here

Husband
Another caller

I'm not at home to anyone

Fortuneteller
I thought you'd all be pleased

To have your fortunes told

Policeman
You are well aware Madame

You're practicing an illegal occupation

It's astonishing what folks will do

To get out of doing an honest day's work

Husband

No hanky-panky in my house please

Fortuneteller *to a spectator*

You Sir will shortly

Give birth to triplets

Husband

Competition already

A Lady Member of the Audience

Madame Fortuneteller

I think my man is two-timing me

Fortuneteller

Keep him in the crock pot

(She climbs on the stage.)

Well I never, an incubator

Husband

If you're the barber give me a haircut

Fortuneteller

The young girls of New York

Pick greengages to eat

All they like is ham from York

That's why they are so sweet

Husband

Parisiennes are nice

115

Much nicer than the rest

If pussies all love mice

We love your pussies best

Fortuneteller

He means your puss-onalities

The People of Zanzibar

You gotta sing from morn till night

And scratch wherever you itch

Feel free to go for black or white

It can be fun to switch

All

Just mind you get it right (x3)

Fortuneteller

Pure and chaste citizens of Zanzibar

Who have no children

Know now that fame and fortune will belong by right

To those who will claim them with armies of infants

*(The **children** start to cry.)*

You who are so fertile

Husband and Policeman

Fertile fertile

Fortuneteller *(to the Husband)*

You'll be a millionaire ten times over

(to the Policeman) You who don't have children

You'll die in abject poverty

Policeman

This is an insult

I arrest you in the name of Zanzibar

Fortuneteller

Laying hands on a woman shame on you

(*Fortuneteller strangles Policeman to death.*)

Husband

Hey my sweet poppet slink roll up to the bar

I'll spin you a tune as I roll your cigar

'Bout the wife of the baker of Zanzibar

Who each seventh year has stolen the car

She sheds her skin by the light of a star

Fortuneteller

This woman she carries a joke too far

Husband

Meanwhile I'm taking you down to the police station you murderess

Therese (*throwing off her headdress*)

Don't you recognize me Husband dear

Husband

Therese or should I say Tiresias

(*The Policeman revives.*)

117

Therese

Tiresias is at present officially

Head of the Army in Room A at City Hall

But keep your hat on

I'm bringing back in a moving van

The piano the violin and the butter dish

And three influential ladies whose lover I've become

Policeman

Thanks for thinking of me

Husband

My general my deputy

Therese, I meant to say

You're as flat-chested as a board

A carpenter's dream

Therese

So what! Let's pick and gather strawberries

And the banana blossoms

Let's hunt elephants on safaris

Like the Zanzibarese

Come and rule the heart of Therese

Husband

Therese

Therese

Throne or tomb no matter what

But this I'm sure of that we've got

To love or I'll die on the spot

<u>Husband</u>

Dear Therese you can't remain

As flat as a board

(He hands her a bouquet of balloons and a basket of balls.)

Here are fresh supplies

<u>Therese</u>

We've both done okay without them

Let's just carry on

<u>Husband</u>

You're right let's not complicate our lives

Let's go and have our soup instead

<u>Therese</u> *(sharing the balloons)*

Fly away birds of my weakness

Go and feed all the children

Of the new population

<u>All</u> *(throwing the balls to the public)*

So sing from morn till night

And scratch wherever you itch

Feel free to go for black or white

It can be fun to switch

Just mind you get it right (4X)

*(Everyone dances. The **Husband** plays the sax for **Therese** leading the **People of Zanzibar** to sing "Two to Tango".)*

119

The People of Zanzibar

You can sail on a ship by yourself

Take a nap or a nip by yourself

You can get into debt on your own

There are a lot of things that you can do alone

Chorus: **But it takes two to tango, two to tango**

Two to really get the feeling of romance

Let's do tango, do to tango

Do the dance of love

The Husband and Therese

You can fight like a champ by yourself (Husband)

You can lick any stamp by yourself (Therese)

You can be very brave on the phone (Husband)

There are a lot of things that you can do alone (Both)

The People of Zanzibar and The Policeman

You can croon to the moon by yourself (The People of Zanzibar)

You can laugh like a loon by yourself (The Policeman)

Spend a lot, smoke some pot on our own (The People of Zanzibar)

There are a lot of things that you can do alone (Both)

Chorus

All

You can haunt any house by yourself (Presto and Lacouf)

Be a man, or a mouse by yourself (The P. of Zanzi and The Policeman)

You can act like a king on a throne (Therese and the Husband)

There are a lot of things that you can do alone (All)

Chorus / Dance break / Bows

All

It takes two

It takes two

Darling it only takes two

Me and you

ENCORE: *"This Is the Time" by Lou Reed*

This is no time to count your blessings
This is no time for private gain
This is the time to put up or shut up
It won't come back this way again

This is no time to swallow anger
This is no time to ignore hate
This is no time to be acting frivolous
Because the time is getting late

(Chorus) There is no time There is no time

There is no time There is no time

Because there's no time, this is the time

This is the time This is the time
This is the time This is the time

This is no time for private vendettas
This is no time to not know who you are
Self-knowledge is a dangerous thing
The freedom of who you are

This is no time to ignore warnings
This is no time to clear the plate
Let's not be sorry after the fact
And let the past become our fate

(Chorus) This is no time to turn away and drink
Or smoke some vials of crack
This is a time to gather force
And take dead aim and attack

This is no time for phony rhetoric
This is no time for political speech
This is a time for action
Because the future's within reach   (Chorus ad infinitum)

FIN

121

INTRODUCTION TO
INTERVIEW or WHO'S AFRAID OF MR. ALBEE?

I met American playwright Edward Albee after directing his one-act play, *Finding the Sun*, for a jury at San Diego State University in 1992. Having been known for tearing into most students' work at the annual jury, all student directors passed on the opportunity. Even though I was only in my second year, I was allowed to take on the project.

After the scene from the play was performed Mr. Albee stood up, turned to the audience, and said, "I just want to begin the discussion by saying I thought that was great." Over the years I became a minor pen-pal with Mr. Albee, sending him odd postcards from time to time. When I was writing and directing a grand opus in my final year at State Mr. Albee advised me to "fail big".

Mr. Albee wrote the extraordinary *Three Tall Women* around the time I moved to New York. I read the script in *American Theatre* magazine and wept. I saw it with my grandmother and aunt, and I ushered many times. Some years later, I traveled twice with Joseph Chaikin to Valdez, Alaska where there was a Playwrights Conference led by Mr. Albee. Finally in 2003 I was granted a residency at Mr. Albee's Montauk retreat called The Barn. In that month, I wrote a song for Mr. Albee called "Who Put the Bomb in the Basement?" which we performed during our thank you dinner. One of my Barn-mates, artist Joan Waltemath, an editor-at-large of *The Brooklyn Rail*, suggested I conduct an interview with Mr. Albee.

I prepared extensively for the interview by studying dozens of previous interviews that had been conducted over fifty years. I saw him on video demolishing reporters that were not quick enough and walking away in disgust.

The night before the interview I realized that I would create a play without actually writing a play and I'd present it with Albeeian style on the page. With all due admiration and respect this play would be an accurate portrayal of the playwright himself, a portrait that is as true as a photograph and as fantastic as life itself.

Interview

or

Who's Afraid of Mr. Albee?

a play in one scene by

Eric "Wally" Wallach

Based on an interview with Edward Albee by Eric Wallach at Mr. Albee's Tribeca loft in New York City on March 15, 2005.

"No one should come to New York to live unless he is willing to be lucky."

- E. B. White, *Here is New York*

THE PLAYERS:

MR. ALBEE

A playwright, 77, dressed in muted earth tones, a moustache, and glasses. His dress and manner would suggest a man younger.

INTERVIEWER

A theatre artist, 33, smartly dressed in his own style, a beard and glasses.

THE SCENE:

Mr. Albee's large Tribeca loft, full of art and African furniture. A leather couch sits off center with a black swivel chair to its left with a large square dark wooden table in front of both. Sunlight pours in through the windows.

(The curtain rises on Mr. Albee's loft. The INTERVIEWER is sitting on the couch looking over his notes. He stops reading, cleans his glasses, goes back to reading. MR. ALBEE enters.)

MR. ALBEE

Good morning.

(The INTERVIEWER gets up and shakes hands with MR. ALBEE.)

INTERVIEWER

Good morning. *(Sitting down again, he sets up his minidisk recorder and microphone between them)* How, uh, how are you today?

(Mr. Albee sits down with a tall glass of iced coffee)

MR. ALBEE

Just fine, nothing new.

INTERVIEWER

No news?

MR. ALBEE

No.

INTERVIEWER

I brought something for you. *(He presents a white box from a brown paper bag)* To say thank you with a little happy 77th birthday thrown in.

MR. ALBEE

Well, thank you.

INTERVIEWER

Some dried cranberries, apricots, and strawberries.

MR. ALBEE

I'll open it later. Would you like some water?

INTERVIEWER

No thanks. *(Knowing full well Mr. Albee hasn't had a drink in thirty years)* You don't do any heavy drinking in the morning?

MR. ALBEE

(Glaring) What?

INTERVIEWER

Do I remember correctly?

MR. ALBEE

I haven't had a drink in thirty years.

INTERVIEWER

That's right. *(Pause)* Did you drink while you wrote, *Who's Afraid of Virginia Woolf*?

MR. ALBEE

(Upset, shakes his head) Now why go *there*? Drinking. Really?!

INTERVIEWER

(Trying) I just, I just wanted to know whether you've witnessed any drunken rehearsals of the play?

MR. ALBEE

Absolutely not, never. No writer, no director, no *actor* can do their work while drunk. You can't do it. You've got to be thinking all the time.

INTERVIEWER

(Looking around) You have no stereo down here?

MR. ALBEE

Why?

INTERVIEWER

I was hoping to hear some Bach. I have no Bach in my music collection. And, uh, in one of your hundreds of interviews you said that you advise your playwrighting students that they should listen to a Bach fugue every morning. What's Bach got?

MR. ALBEE *(overlapping)*

I never said every morning. I said that a writer should listen to a fugue before they begin their writing. To clear up the mind. *(With the slightest of grins)* You should try it.

INTERVIEWER *(repositioning the microphone)*

I will. *(Silence)* It was great seeing you last Saturday night at your first New York performance of *Who's Afraid of Virginia Woolf?* From where I was sitting, I could see you in your house right box, legs propped up on a chair in front of you. I never saw you take your eyes off the stage.

MR. ALBEE

Where else should I be looking?

INTERVIEWER

You never once looked at the audience.

MR. ALBEE

I can hear them.

INTERVIEWER

The audience was raucous. The laughter was constant through the first act.

MR. ALBEE

Were you watching them or watching me?

INTERVIEWER

I was watching the *play*.

MR. ALBEE

(Deep breath) Preview audiences are usually younger, they have more energy, they get more involved … they at least haven't come to the theatre after drinking four martinis.

INTERVIEWER

Yeah. *(Pause)* Just to let you know, I'm still working on the screenplay that I began at The Barn in August of 2003. I'm now on Draft Six, Act Two.

MR. ALBEE

Draft six?

INTERVIEWER

The screenplay keeps changing course.

MR. ALBEE

I'd worry about that. You lose your spontaneity. You start trying to make things happen as opposed to letting it come out naturally.

INTERVIEWER

The theatre editor at *The Brooklyn Rail* suggested that I begin the interview with a brief account of your accomplishments to bring the reader in. *(Pause)* Um, should I do it or would you like to?

MR. ALBEE

You want me to?! Not *me*. And I hope you don't expect me to *listen*.

INTERVIEWER

It'll be painless.

MR. ALBEE *(Reluctantly)*

All right.

INTERVIEWER

(Reading slowly from the page with a smidgen of Howard Cosell inflection) Mr. Albee, your playwrighting career spans almost fifty years, your contributions to the art of theatre include such plays as *The Zoo Story*, *Who's Afraid of Virginia Woolf? A Delicate Balance*, *Tiny Alice*, *Seascape*, *Three Tall Women* and *The Goat, or Who is Sylvia?* - you have peeled back the skin and sucked the marrow of human experience. You are truly one of the greatest dramatists of our time. Maybe, of all time.

MR. ALBEE

(In a low voice) So you say. Sounds nice.

INTERVIEWER

(Probing) How do you deal with your celebrity?

MR. ALBEE

What celebrity? If I stay out of midtown or the theatre no one recognizes me, I can go about my business normally.

INTERVIEWER

You're very lucky then. *(Pause)* I was remembering last night, about when we first met some fourteen years ago at San Diego State University, I was remembering some great advice that you gave me that I still hold dear.

MR. ALBEE

What did I say?

INTERVIEWER

You told me to "Fail big."

MR. ALBEE

Why else would you attempt writing in the first place?

INTERVIEWER

Speaking of failing big, you were a part of a jury that had come to the university for years to watch and criticize the student's presentations. Your reputation proceeded you. All the students who had witnessed past juries saw work ripped effortlessly to shreds …

MR. ALBEE

I was never *mean*.

INTERVIEWER

They say it happened every time … and that you were brilliant but cruel.

MR. ALBEE

I was never cruel. *(Smiling)* Honest and accurate, yes, but never cruel, no.

INTERVIEWER

(Glancing at his notes)

I tried to see the connection between you and Antonin Artaud which some academics suggest in books I've read. But when I discovered your work, I realized very quickly that Artaud is Artaud *(Dramatic pause)* and Edward Albee is Edward Albee.

MR. ALBEE

That's the way it should be.

INTERVIEWER

(Checking his list of questions)

You first saw *Who's Afraid of Virginia Woolf?* 43 years ago. Few writers have had the opportunity to see their work develop over so many years, do you feel it resonates today in ways that it didn't when you first wrote it?

MR. ALBEE

It's the same play.

129

INTERVIEWER

Yes, but has the audience changed? Back in the 60's the government was lying and deceiving the people, but they weren't as aware of it as they are now. Right?

MR. ALBEE

(Overlapping)

Now people know the truth … but prefer the lies.

INTERVIEWER

You've said that *Virginia Woolf* is about the "failure of the principals of the American Revolution" -- what did you mean by that?

MR. ALBEE

I said that to confuse the academics. But yes, Nick is named after Nikita Khrushchev who was threatening our country at the time. George and Martha are named after the Washingtons. Technology was threatening human expression, art, culture.

INTERVIEWER

Uh huh.

MR. ALBEE

You know Honey's name isn't Honey, right? *(Pause)* That's just what Nick *calls* her.

INTERVIEWER

Funny.

MR. ALBEE

And the only way you know *his* name, is if you *read the play*.

INTERVIEWER

(Nodding) Oh, no one calls him by his name.

MR. ALBEE

Right.

INTERVIEWER

Why is Honey so wild for violence?

MR. ALBEE

She just is. That's her nature.

INTERVIEWER *(Shifting gears)*

You quit your job at Western Union in 1957 and in three weeks you finished your first play, can you describe the man that sat down to the typewriter to write *The Zoo Story*?

MR. ALBEE

I don't remember. I think I was still working at Western Union when I wrote it. I quit my job to go to Europe.

INTERVIEWER

For the opening?

MR. ALBEE

That's right.

INTERVIEWER

You seem to love shocking your audience. In all your plays you find a way to unnerve your audience into the world of the play.

MR. ALBEE

I don't like terms like that. *Shock.* I don't want to shock; I want to *involve*.

INTERVIEWER

You start *The Play About the Baby* with two nude actors running around the stage. That's not shocking?

131

MR. ALBEE

In the stage directions I wrote, "Nakedly." Nakedly. *(Hidden smile)* They weren't nude, unless they wanted to be.

INTERVIEWER

What are your expectations of your audience?

MR. ALBEE

I want them to be *sober*, listening and they need to have a willingness to suspend their disbelief.

INTERVIEWER

When you direct, you tell your actors, "Do what you want, as long as you get to what I want." What is it that you want from your actors?

MR. ALBEE

I want real characters and real actors living in a three-dimensional world.

INTERVIEWER

What do you want when you curate art shows?

MR. ALBEE

I want space. Unencumbered. Nothing to pull away the attention of the viewer. Space to look at each work without distraction.

INTERVIEWER

How do you encourage writers to discover their own true voice?

MR. ALBEE

True voice? What's that? You can't teach it at all; it's inherent or not.

INTERVIEWER

Who do you find funny?

MR. ALBEE

I used to find politics funny. Not anymore. It's real scary these days.

INTERVIEWER

I couldn't agree more. *(Pause)* Well, then, who makes you laugh?

MR. ALBEE *(Thinks for a moment)*

What do you want, a list?

INTERVIEWER

No.

MR. ALBEE

Well, I could say, Henny Youngman, you know Borsht Belt, one-liners. And Myron Cohen, the dialect comedian. He did different voices, different dialects. You should get a record, you'll like it.

INTERVIEWER

Great. Um, in what ways have your plays had a cathartic effect on your life?

MR. ALBEE

It hasn't really. *(Pause)* Well, except I suppose exorcising my adopted mother in *Three Tall Women*. *(Grinning)* Haven't thought of her since. So, there's that.

INTERVIEWER

You've seen so much theatre over the years, can you tell me about the moments in the theatre that you savor?

MR. ALBEE

I've seen a lot of things and I don't remember the details at all. It's gone.

INTERVIEWER

Will society ever stop needing new plays?

MR. ALBEE

No. Will they still *see* plays is another question.

INTERVIEWER

How will theatre adapt itself if it's going to remain essential?

MR. ALBEE

We'll always need storytellers. *(His cell phone rings)* Is that all your questions? Did we get through it? *(He gets up and walks away)* Hello?

INTERVIEWER

I think so. *(He checks through his notes then pauses his minidisk recorder)* Oh my god. *(He starts panicking, pushing buttons in silence.)* Wow.

Note: Now the script is a verbatim transcription of the interview. No additions or edits were made from what actually occurred.

MR. ALBEE

(Into phone) Alright, goodbye. *(He walks back slowly and sits)* What? You didn't get it?

INTERVIEWER

(To himself)

Unbelievable … ok. So, we're starting back … unbelievable. *(Slams his hand down then takes a moment to look at* MR. ALBEE*)* It happens sometimes that, ah, you can't record the beautiful things. Some moments can't be recorded.

MR. ALBEE

Well, you remember all my answers to your questions – my *evasions*.

INTERVIEWER

Yeah? *(Doubtful)* For the most part. I could get some refreshers though. *(He looks over his notes, nodding)* Yeah, for the most part. *(Bites his lip, pained)* Would you mind me writing your lines?

134

MR. ALBEE

No, go ahead, just send them to me, of course. *(Being helpful)* In this situation I would type something up and send it to me so that I can correct my mistakes. And yours. *(Laughs)*

INTERVIEWER

Right. *(It's sinking in)* Oh that's good, that's *great* … it'll be fun. Um, I ah, that's great, how much more fun is that? I really, last night, I had a revelation about the interview in that, ah, it's going to be *you* and me and we're … it's going to emerge, like your plays, like you talk about your process. You know? It's not, what do *I* want and I'm gonna come in and I'm gonna … *(Pounds something out)* but that something will emerge, something will have happened.

MR. ALBEE

Well, something happened.

INTERVIEWER

Yeah. You know what's funny is that *The Brooklyn Rail* said that they would transcribe the interview for me. Then I would be *(Snap)* done with the interview and … ha ha, right? It's gonna be something else.

MR. ALBEE

(Suppressed chuckle) Very funny.

INTERVIEWER

But this is - will be a dialogue that I'll have to try recreating in some way.

MR. ALBEE

Yeah.

INTERVIEWER

And we'll, and with your help … *(Stunned)* though, Mr. Albee … I have a very quick deadline.

MR. ALBEE

When's that?

INTERVIEWER

(Intense) The twenty-second. In a week's time.

MR. ALBEE

Oh? *(Grinning)* Hmm.

INTERVIEWER

Which means that I bike home right now and get out as much as I can remember and get it back to you quite quickly. Do you mind?

MR. ALBEE

I don't mind.

INTERVIEWER

(Sincerely surprised) Really? I appreciate that. It'll be fun.

MR. ALBEE

E-mail it or fax it, whatever you do.

INTERVIEWER

Do you? What e-mail?

MR. ALBEE

I don't know what my e-mail number *is*. The fax is 212.529.1717.

INTERVIEWER

I love it. As much as I checked it and made sure, it always happens to me—it's not a surprise when technology doesn't come through.

MR. ALBEE

Of course not, I know.

INTERVIEWER

I love it, because what we had was real. What we were experiencing is real.

MR. ALBEE *(Plainly)*

And why should anybody else get in on it.

INTERVIEWER

Absolutely.

MR. ALBEE

Exactly.

INTERVIEWER

It's ours. *(Smiles)* I really thank you.

MR. ALBEE

You've got all those questions; you seem to remember all my answers —my evasions.

INTERVIEWER

I think so. You didn't evade at all, but you're a lot funnier than I'm going to be able to… so I hope you're gonna be able to bring some of the good… *(Hatcha, snap, snap)*

MR. ALBEE

That's the trouble; humor very, very, very seldom transcribes.

INTERVIEWER

No, that's true.

MR. ALBEE

Practically never.

INTERVIEWER

(Annoyed) But an interview, it's meant to be read just like your plays…

MR. ALBEE

Because comic timing cannot be transcribed onto paper.

INTERVIEWER

(Pause) You try sometimes in your stage directions and things.

MR. ALBEE

Yeah, if I know a certain number of beats before a line, I know when it works and when it doesn't. But an interview's comic timing cannot be transcribed.

INTERVIEWER

(Shaking his head) This is going to be really hard. It *has* been for the past week, reading and re-reading your plays and interviews. Ah. So it continues.

MR. ALBEE

Poor you.

INTERVIEWER

For me. Yeah *(Quietly recognizing)* poor me.

MR. ALBEE

(Correcting him)

Not - *for* you, *poor* you.

INTERVIEWER

(Nodding)

Yeah, I know, I gotchya. Poor me. *(Forcing a smile)* It's been great. *(Pause)* It's been great and I will enjoy trying to, uh …

MR. ALBEE

So, is it still broken? *(Points at the minidisk recorder)*

INTERVIEWER

No, it's rolling now. Um, I wonder if you would mind if I could just go back through my notes and make sure… What's funny is that I didn't keep to any order. *(Turning pages)*

MR. ALBEE *(Quick)*

No of course not.

INTERVIEWER

Um, mhmm, uhuh, yeah, you're going to have to write your own great line; "Don't get into the drinking!" Oh. *(Serious disappointment)* What I was so excited about, with the transcribing, is that I could've left it just real, what it was. And it could've just been an eardrop…

MR. ALBEE

Now you're gonna have to be literary.

INTERVIEWER

Ugh, it's the worst!

MR. ALBEE

Oh, we'll just have to revise six times.

INTERVIEWER

Ugh, I find it a little depressing because I do like what's real in an interview and somehow, we're going to have to write it. That's a *crap*…

MR. ALBEE

Well, you're gonna have to be a playwright.

INTERVIEWER

I find it very hard to be a playwright, Mr. Albee. That's why I'm not. I'm really a director, ya know? I stopped. The only time and reason I wrote was so I could direct it. I wanted to see something. I'm not a playwright like you, wanting to craft words and characters and moments. I like working rehearsal. I like making things happen on stage.

MR. ALBEE

Well so do I.

INTERVIEWER

Yeah, well I'm sure you do. *(Pause)* All your moments. *(Pause)* So … so visceral. *(Long pause, turns through pages)* Mmm, wow, mmm. What was your great response to ah, "You're truly one of the greatest dramatists of our time."?

MR. ALBEE *(Remembering or writing)*

I don't think in those terms.

INTERVIEWER

(Fake laugh, sigh)

You had some good ones, ooh. *(Takes a breath)* All right, that's the past. Now we're now. Um, *(Mumbles)* wow. *(Somewhat cheerful)* Oh, I like it that way. That's the way it should be. *(Trying to remember again)* You said… Do you remember the question?

MR. ALBEE

Nope.

INTERVIEWER

Artaud is Artaud. And Edward Albee is Edward Albee. "And that's the way is should be." Um. *(He scribbles and giggles)* Gosh, all that stuff about Nick and Honey… *(Sucking it up)* Ok, I'm not going to do this in front of you. I'll be able to do it. *(Thinking again)* You said something about being, not inventing, um… *(Pause)* speci … specificity. Being specific with your words… *(Mumbles)* oh this is going to be rough…

MR. ALBEE

I don't know what you're talking about.

INTERVIEWER

Ah, it's ok. *(Pause, a breath)* I love it. I love the time that we've had. I wonder, I probably don't have a lot more. *(Scribbling more notes)*

MR. ALBEE

Keep going.

INTERVIEWER

Thank you.

MR. ALBEE

I mean, you're spending most of your time sitting here kvetching. I mean …

INTERVIEWER

Exactly. So I'm going to get over it. Right, you were accurate… students… *(Scribbling some more notes)*

MR. ALBEE

That's the joke, the Jewish joke about the deaf dog.

INTERVIEWER

What? *(Finally puts down his pen)* The deaf dog?

MR. ALBEE

The deaf dog. Old Jewish man took his dog to the vet, said there's something wrong with it. The vet examined the dog. The dog seemed fine. And uh, it's a talking dog, by the way. And the guy said, you wanna see what's wrong with the dog. And he looked at the dog and said, "Fetch!" The dog walked away a few paces and said, "You never take me out, you never give me good food, you make me sit here all the time, you never talk to me, you're never nice to me." *(Laughter)* And he said, "Don't you see? The dog's deaf. Can't tell the difference between 'fetch' and 'kvetch.'" *(Chuckles)* So, you're sitting here kvetching instead of fetching.

INTERVIEWER

Indeed, indeed. Was that a Henny Youngman?

141

MR. ALBEE

It should be. *(After a thought)* It's too long, he did one-liners. Ya know?

INTERVIEWER

Yeah, yeah.

MR. ALBEE

"Take my wife, please!" routines.

INTERVIEWER

You love the one-liner, huh?

MR. ALBEE

Mmm hmm. Often, it's good, it's really funny and damaging and dangerous.

INTERVIEWER

You're able to get your... Your economy of words is astounding the way you chisel your scripts so that there's no word in excess.

MR. ALBEE

I hope not. I learn that from people like Beckett and Chekhov.

INTERVIEWER

(Pause)

Rhythm?

MR. ALBEE

By wanting to be a composer and knowing a great deal about music. And understanding that a playwright notates the same way a composer does. Half notes, quarter notes, dotted eighth notes. Fast, slow, loud, soft.

142

INTERVIEWER

Do you hear *Virginia Woolf* as a quartet all the time?

MR. ALBEE

Oh sure.

INTERVIEWER

What were the qualities of Bill Irwin and Kathleen Turner that made you gravitate to them?

MR. ALBEE

Contrasting manners. Overboard for Kathleen, underneath to the same goal for Bill. Intelligence on the part of both of them. *(Pause)* I think Bill will be a revelation to people.

INTERVIEWER

How so?

MR. ALBEE

Well, because ya know, everybody knows him just as a clown. They've never seen him perform Beckett, as I have. Good actor.

INTERVIEWER

Great actor. He's able to hit everything naturally and realistically in a way, but perfectly in time.

MR. ALBEE

Yea, it's a matter of timing. *(Nodding)*

INTERVIEWER

(Long awkward silence) I like to say, God is timing.

MR. ALBEE

Who?

143

INTERVIEWER

Who? Who, hmm, who is right. Do you think that we've been a victim of this God and this, this creation of God? Ah, man.

MR. ALBEE

You mean, man creating God in his own image?

INTERVIEWER

Yeah

MR. ALBEE

It's so preposterous and I don't really see what you can say about it. The only god that can be worshipped is that which cannot be conceived of or imagined. *Tiny Alice* takes care of all those things.

INTERVIEWER

Indeed, it does. Do you think we'll ever get over God?

MR. ALBEE

No. Of course not.

INTERVIEWER

I know it's been years, but …

MR. ALBEE

God won't let us. *(Laughs)*

INTERVIEWER

(Understanding) The smoke screen.

MR. ALBEE

(Nodding) Sure.

INTERVIEWER

(Pause)

But, I think about the future, I mean the future future, and… Don't we know enough by now? Don't we know that war is insane, is a money-making machine fueled on the lives of innocent people?

MR. ALBEE

Well don't forget that last refuge of scoundrels—patriotism.

INTERVIEWER

Hmm, who wrote that?

MR. ALBEE

I can't remember, somebody good.

INTERVIEWER

(Chuckle) Hmm, yeah.

MR. ALBEE

The more we learn, the better we get at self-deception.

INTERVIEWER

(Long pause) It's healthy. Denial. Denial is quite, hmm, self-deception, it's distance … well I don't know what. What is it?

MR. ALBEE

What is what?

INTERVIEWER

Self-deception.

MR. ALBEE

It's something we invent so that we don't have to think about things. *(Pause)* That's the whole point of *Who's Afraid of Virginia Woolf?*. *The Iceman Cometh,* O'Neil says you have to have false illusions in order to survive. Right? *Who's Afraid of Virginia Woolf?* says it's ok to have false illusions as long as you know they're false. The problem comes when you start believing them.

INTERVIEWER

Do you think at the end of *Who's Afraid of Virginia Woolf?* … it seems like, uh, Martha admits the fear of the truth?

MR. ALBEE

Yes. When he says to her, "Who's afraid of Virginia Woolf?", she says, "I am George." She's afraid of living life without the false illusions.

INTERVIEWER

(Pause) And you leave it there.

MR. ALBEE

Of course.

INTERVIEWER

Blackout.

MR. ALBEE

That's the way it should be left.

INTERVIEWER

Absolutely.

MR. ALBEE

Mm hmm. *(Correcting the INTERVIEWER)* Slow fade.

INTERVIEWER

Thank you. I wonder, uh, do you think about …

MR. ALBEE

(More accurately) Medium fade.

INTERVIEWER

(Chuckle) Medium, yeah. Thank you. Do… You don't. *(Smiling)* I know you don't. Do you ever think about your characters' lives *after* the play?

MR. ALBEE

No. But it was very interesting when I wrote *Home Life*.

INTERVIEWER

Oh, that's your new play? A first act to *The Zoo Story*?

MR. ALBEE

I had to think about my character's life before *The Zoo Story*. It's quite different. It's not just thinking about it after the fact. I decided I wanted to know what was going on for Peter at home before he went to the park. So, I started writing it and I realized that after 45 years or so I still knew who Peter was and I still knew who his wife was.

INTERVIEWER

Right and the two kids…

MR. ALBEE

The whole thing. I still knew who they *were*.

INTERVIEWER

(Interested)

Do you have the birds?

MR. ALBEE

There are birds, they're not on stage. Kids aren't on stage either.

INTERVIEWER

It's a two-person? With the wife.

MR. ALBEE

Mmm, Anne.

INTERVIEWER

(Chuckles) Anne? Where did that come from?

MR. ALBEE

That's her name. *(Laughs)*

INTERVIEWER

(Big laugh then pause)

Are we ever going to see it in New York?

MR. ALBEE

I hope so, sure.

INTERVIEWER

When are we going to be able to *read* it?

MR. ALBEE

Probably after we see it in New York.

INTERVIEWER

Uh huh. *(Laughter)* When'd you finish?

MR. ALBEE

A year ago.

INTERVIEWER

What are you waiting for?

MR. ALBEE

Aaah, proper production in New York.

INTERVIEWER

And what is that? I mean, who's responsible …

MR. ALBEE

It will happen.

INTERVIEWER

Uhuh, exactly, it will happen, it will happen. *(Long pause)* It's another shocking turn for Mr. Albee to… to write a previous act. It's *terrific* really.

MR. ALBEE

I couldn't have done it if it wasn't there.

INTERVIEWER

Indeed, indeed.

MR. ALBEE

And I couldn't have written Peter in *The Zoo Story* unless I'd *known* what his home life was like. I just hadn't had the need to focus on it. But it was still there.

INTERVIEWER

What was the need now to focus there?

MR. ALBEE

I thought it would be interesting to do.

INTERVIEWER

Like most of your plays.

MR. ALBEE

Yes, most of all I was getting tired of having to approve of other plays that people wanted to do with *The Zoo Story*. And so if I have *this*, I could do the two of them together. It's all one play. *Home Life* and *The Zoo Story* have become *Peter and Jerry*. That's the title.

INTERVIEWER

Right. So no more *American Dream* and *Zoo Story*.

MR. ALBEE

No.

INTERVIEWER

It can now finally live as a full length.

MR. ALBEE
(Quick)

As a what?

INTERVIEWER

(Laughs) Sorry *(Getting it right)* as a longer night of theatre.

MR. ALBEE

That's right. *(Notices something)* What is that spray can you have there?

INTERVIEWER

(Picking up and showing his silver thermos to MR. ALBEE*)* It's a thermos. I haven't used it yet.

MR. ALBEE

Oh, it's a thermos. I thought you were going to spray the loft or something.

INTERVIEWER

No. *(Taking a drink)* How do you end Act One?

MR. ALBEE

Uh, where it should be. Peter leaving the apartment. To go to the park. It takes intermission for him to get there.

INTERVIEWER

Uh ha, that's great, and then he arrives. *(Wondering)* What book is he reading?

MR. ALBEE

I don't know, that's up to him. Up to the actor. I don't want to see the title.

INTERVIEWER

Uh huh. It doesn't matter.

MR. ALBEE

I mean, it's not going to say John Grisham or anything awful like that.

INTERVIEWER

But he does bring a book?

MR. ALBEE

Yes, of course.

                    INTERVIEWER

To sit at the park.

                    MR. ALBEE
               (Shrugging shoulders simply)
Sure, of course. It's the book he's reading.

                    INTERVIEWER

(Chuckle and a smile) Is he …

                    MR. ALBEE
Peter.

                    INTERVIEWER
Peter.

                    MR. ALBEE
Is he what?

                    INTERVIEWER
Uh, is he a *dupe* for you?

                    MR. ALBEE
A what?

                    INTERVIEWER
(Clearer) A dupe. *(Seriously)* Do you set him up to tear him down?

                    MR. ALBEE
Don't be insulting. *(Smiles)*

152

INTERVIEWER

Really? *(Laughing)*

MR. ALBEE

Yes of course. He's a real person. He's having his life and he makes the mistake of talking to Jerry. Of course, he learns a *great deal* by talking to Jerry. He's probably going to be a quite *different person* by the end of *The Zoo Story*. And that will affect his future and his life with his wife and everything. Yeah. A *dupe*?

INTERVIEWER

Listen, it seems to me that you, your plays, you set up worlds and you tear them down.

MR. ALBEE

No *(Pointedly)* the *characters* tear them down.

INTERVIEWER

(Suppressed gut laugh) What about that moment in *Delicate Balance* when the neighbors come over and say, 'we're going to stay'?

MR. ALBEE

That was interesting.

INTERVIEWER

Horrifying.

MR. ALBEE

Obviously, I decided they were going to do that, but I was quite surprised when they said it.

INTERVIEWER

I bet.

MR. ALBEE

(Coughs)

Same way that with *Three Tall Women* I didn't know the boy was going to come in, in the second act, until I wrote the boy enters.

INTERVIEWER

You're like, "Look who's here."

MR. ALBEE

Well look who's here. It's a four-character play, my goodness. But obviously I'd decided. I hadn't told myself.

INTERVIEWER

Self-deception.

MR. ALBEE

No, you learn things when you need to. He didn't need to come in until that point, so why would I inform myself until that point?

INTERVIEWER

Right. Right. Did you like that revival of *Delicate Balance*, the last one? With, with that sweater, the sweater of the neighbor, the woman *(Gesturing turtleneck)* -

MR. ALBEE

Oh, I guess she didn't like her neck.

INTERVIEWER

It was … it was … I mean, I felt so *(Choking himself)* for her. I mean like, she looked like Winnie a little bit. You know?

MR. ALBEE

Hmm … Yeah, it was a good production.

INTERVIEWER

I had front row seats for it. *(He purrs like a sexy cat)* Do you like sitting in the back or the front, or in the middle or on the side?

MR. ALBEE

As long as I can be alone.

INTERVIEWER

I can't imagine you sitting in the theatre and weeping over your plays.

MR. ALBEE

Of course not, I'm too busy making sure they're being performed correctly.

INTERVIEWER

Then why the need to be alone?

MR. ALBEE

I don't like distraction. That's why that box is fine. *(Glares)* Except some people could look at you.

INTERVIEWER

Sorry.

MR. ALBEE

I'll wear a beard and funny hair next time.

INTERVIEWER

I was the only one who knew. *(Pause)* You didn't see me?

MR. ALBEE

Did you wave?

INTERVIEWER

I did. I almost heckled you after the show. I almost said, "Mr. Albee, you rock!" The play rocks.

MR. ALBEE

That's not a heckle.

INTERVIEWER

No. Ahh, is a heckle derogatory? Not derogatory …

MR. ALBEE

Yes, it is usually.

INTERVIEWER

It's another great Yiddish word.

MR. ALBEE

Is it?

INTERVIEWER

I'm assuming, actually. Sorry. But I'm assuming that *(Listening to the word)* heckle, *heckle*.

MR. ALBEE

It sounds German. *(Admitting)* Well, a lot of Yiddish is German.

INTERVIEWER

It feels like a word that probably came up in the New York Yiddish Theatre.

MR. ALBEE

There was a Hegel and there was a Heckle, by the way.

INTERVIEWER

(Laughing)

Is that right?

MR. ALBEE

There's a Heckle there somewhere. Maybe he was a scientist. I don't know.

INTERVIEWER

The act of going to the theatre, back when … *(Thinking)* probably before your time …

MR. ALBEE

I didn't go to the theatre before my time.

INTERVIEWER

I know. But people *did*, and they threw vegetables and they yelled back at the stage and they were involved in it as a sporting event, the way they could jeer it … by the time *you* come along …

MR. ALBEE

Spontaneity out the window.

INTERVIEWER

Umm. *(Searching)* Beckett came more from that place, more from a place, from Vaudeville, which I feel informs his work in the relationship with the audience, that it's really happening in the space.

MR. ALBEE

Yeah, too much is made of it, that's why *Godot* is not as good as most of his other plays. He didn't have the comedic elements under total control yet.

INTERVIEWER

But if the actors find it, then it's a winner.

MR. ALBEE

Yeah, it's fine, but it's still, a little excessive.

INTERVIEWER

What is?

MR. ALBEE

The play's not solid.

INTERVIEWER

No. It just goes *(Makes a trippy 'wawa' sound)*. He's constantly…

MR. ALBEE

I just find that his craft wasn't under total control yet.

INTERVIEWER

There's some moments right there at the end of your play, you end your play *Who's Afraid of Virginia Woolf?* a little like *Godot*, with your: Well, shall we go? Yes, let's go.

MR. ALBEE

I wouldn't be surprised.

INTERVIEWER

Yeah, I wouldn't be surprised either.

MR. ALBEE

It's like the ending of a lot of good pieces of music.

INTERVIEWER

That… It's something with stillness and movement still happening together, the duality-

MR. ALBEE

Yeah, I would like to think that I get my… my moments from good people.

INTERVIEWER

(Shift)

You got to meet Beckett.

MR. ALBEE

Yes.

INTERVIEWER

What did you take from him?

MR. ALBEE

They were casual meetings. He was a gentle, nice man.

INTERVIEWER

Another man of the theatre though. You shared a love.

MR. ALBEE

Well, we didn't talk about our *craft* or anything. I don't remember *what* we talked about.

INTERVIEWER

But you got on?

MR. ALBEE

Yes. I wasn't sitting at his feet or so to speak.

INTERVIEWER

Of course not. And he enjoyed *your* plays? Two men with completely singular visions of their… meaning the manifestation of your theatre is all your own. There's no other laws.

MR. ALBEE

Well, there shouldn't be.

INTERVIEWER

There shouldn't be, but I tell you that there *are* playwrights who think …

MR. ALBEE

I told my playwrighting students, you have to write, and not only do you have to *see* the first play you've ever seen, but every time you *write* a play, you have to *write the first play that's ever been written.* How else can you be individual?

INTERVIEWER

Do you like the quality of amnesia in your life? Waking up as if it's the first day and living it as if it's your last?

MR. ALBEE

Well, I think that's nice. It probably helps with the encroaching Alzheimer's anyway.

INTERVIEWER

(Disagreeing) You are sharper than any blade around. You know it and I know it.

MR. ALBEE

Well, the only comforting thing is that they say that if you know what Alzheimer's is called, you don't have it.

INTERVIEWER *(Laughs)*

In the interviews… I've read that no playwrights are inspiring you right now.

MR. ALBEE

That's nonsense.

160

INTERVIEWER

Is that nonsense?

MR. ALBEE

I'm always taking in nourishment from what other people do. You learn from people's successes and mistakes. You learn what to do and what not to do. And everything relates to your craft.

INTERVIEWER

You spend so many hours in the theatre.

MR. ALBEE

Yeah.

INTERVIEWER

Is it all right?

MR. ALBEE

It's very boring.

INTERVIEWER

Yeah, sometimes. And sometimes, I'm sure you get up and leave if it's not happening for you? Or do you stick it out?

MR. ALBEE

Yeah, I do. *(The cell phone rings again)* I'll be right back.

(MR. ALBEE *gets up. The* INTERVIEWER *pauses the minidisk recorder and scribbles some more notes. When* MR. ALBEE *returns, the* INTERVIEWER *unpauses.)*

INTERVIEWER

(Like a radio announcer) Welcome back.

161

MR. ALBEE *(Taken aback)*

What?

INTERVIEWER

Welcome back.

MR. ALBEE

Okay.

INTERVIEWER *(Big breath)*

Could you tell me again what makes Bach such a good thing to clear the brain?

MR. ALBEE

Clarity, order, inevitability.

INTERVIEWER

Thank you. I appreciate that. That's what I was looking for.

MR. ALBEE

I think that's what a play should be about too. That's the difference between a good play and a bad play. The inevitable verses the arbitrary.

INTERVIEWER

What do you mean?

MR. ALBEE

No matter how surprising a play is, it should always be inevitable.

INTERVIEWER

The course is set.

MR. ALBEE

Uh huh. But after you've finished it, it was never, say I know what was going to happen, but whatever happens, you have to know that it could have been different but the way everything was, the way the people were, the way the situation was… *(Sigh)* it was inevitable.

INTERVIEWER

It's true. All your plays, all your plays are inevitable, from the curtain coming up, you don't know it, but by the end …

MR. ALBEE

Yeah well, a play is a set of parentheses around events.

INTERVIEWER

I wonder what events are *(Changes direction)* Another question. I remember the last time I was here, nine years ago, you told me that you were working on a play about Andre Gide.

MR. ALBEE

Not *about* Andre Gide, he was in the title. The title was, *I Think Back Now On Andre Gide*.

INTERVIEWER

What happened to that play?

MR. ALBEE

(Simply) The title is still there.

INTERVIEWER

And it's still brewing.

MR. ALBEE

Yeah. The play I'm writing *now* is a different title, a different play.

INTERVIEWER *(Quietly hoping)*

Could you tell me a little?

MR. ALBEE

Nope.

INTERVIEWER

(Understanding) It has to remain a secret.

MR. ALBEE

Well, somebody may steal it. Also, I don't know.

INTERVIEWER

How could somebody steal an Edward Albee play?

MR. ALBEE

Steal an idea.

INTERVIEWER

Ahhh… It's that good, eh?

MR. ALBEE

Sure.

INTERVIEWER

You'll let it brew for a while then you'll start work on it in Montauk?

MR. ALBEE

Yeah.

INTERVIEWER

Do you like reading plays?

MR. ALBEE

Yeah, sure. It's more comfortable than seeing them.

INTERVIEWER

It is, isn't it? You can put them down for a second ... *(Smiling)* or longer. Um, there was a real question that I haven't asked you yet. Ahh ... Do you think that plays could, um, change form in any way? Could it exist outside of lights up and blackout?

MR. ALBEE

Where would they exist? They exist already as literature. They can be read.

INTERVIEWER

Indeed. The question I was going to ask was, would breaking the form somehow-

ALBEE

What?

INTERVIEWER

Meaning that you write a play written around a given theme and it could be rearranged, maybe it doesn't go from A to Z?

MR. ALBEE

Well, everything has to go from its beginning to its end.

INTERVIEWER

Yes, but can in performance, can it rearrange itself?

MR. ALBEE

I don't think so. No. Think of a composer.

INTERVIEWER

True. But I'm thinking about the *live* experience.

MR. ALBEE

The aesthetic experience, the intellectual experience, the emotional experience have all got to commence and end. They've got to go from one place to another. They have lots of ways to get from one place to another, but they must get from one place to another. So why would you want them to go in any other fashion?

INTERVIEWER

Somehow, to include the audience...

MR. ALBEE *(Overlapping)*

What's wrong with the mathematical equation working itself out?

INTERVIEWER

I think I'm asking about randomness and the live experience.

MR. ALBEE

Well then, let the actors improvise and that would be a different kind of play, totally, and I wouldn't take credit for it.

INTERVIEWER

Right. Would you enjoy a play like that?

MR. ALBEE

I don't know. I've seen improvisatorial scenes in plays and sometimes they work. Depends on how good the improvisers are.

INTERVIEWER

At the end of the day, it comes down to dialogue. How are the words.

MR. ALBEE

Of course. Things go from a place to a place it seems to me.

INTERVIEWER

(Pointing at a painting)

This piece here reminds me of Joan.

(The cell phone rings again. MR. ALBEE answers it. The INTERVIEWER gets up and wanders around looking at the art.)

MR. ALBEE *(Into his cell phone)*

Hello? Where are you now? Uh huh. I can hear you perfectly well, can you hear me? Oh … The Butterfield will take a little time … *(The INTERVIEWER laughs heartily at an art piece then quiets)* I did? … Nope… I never had one… He was out at my foundation… We are? If it's going to stop, yes. Don't rush though. … Okay… bid higher… yeah, let the action go. *(Long silence)* Okay. Okay… Okay… Nope. Thanks. That's it… kay. Bye bye. *(He hangs up)*

INTERVIEWER

(Walks back and sits down) I love your collection.

MR. ALBEE

Thank you.

INTERVIEWER

It's not decorative.

MR. ALBEE

No, no it's not.

INTERVIEWER *(Careful phrasing)*

It has a beginning and an end, and you can stand away from it and take it in.

MR. ALBEE *(Approving)*

Good.

INTERVIEWER

I like the underwear piece.

MR. ALBEE

I think the artist painted it about AIDS.

INTERVIEWER

(Looking at it from afar) I would describe it as almost six feet tall by four?

MR. ALBEE

It's more than that. I would say it's eight feet by four by five.

INTERVIEWER

(Continuing) With about two dozen pairs of briefs stuck flat to the canvas which has been fully painted black.

MR. ALBEE

How can you have a *pair* of briefs?

INTERVIEWER

That's a very good question.

MR. ALBEE

You can have a pair of socks because those are two.

INTERVIEWER

That's very true, but I don't think I've misspoken. We do refer to briefs as a pair of briefs or even a pair of pants.

MR. ALBEE

Well, that's a mistake, isn't it?

INTERVIEWER

Well, where did that come from?

MR. ALBEE

I don't know.

INTERVIEWER

I don't know either.

MR. ALBEE

It's just wrong.

INTERVIEWER

It's just wrong. The English language sometimes is just absolutely wrong. Which makes it funny. Yeah. In *Who's Afraid of Virginia Woolf?* you're constantly playing language like that.

MR. ALBEE

Yes, my characters are.

INTERVIEWER

(Corrected)

Your characters, thank you. You must have a delightful time at it? Again, I don't have the image of you writing and…

MR. ALBEE

Chuckling?

INTERVIEWER

Well, you may chuckle, yeah?

MR. ALBEE

I chuckle occasionally.

INTERVIEWER

I'm sure, but you don't weep.

MR. ALBEE

No.

INTERVIEWER

You don't write a line and go *(Crying)* oohh?

MR. ALBEE

Oh no, come on. No.

INTERVIEWER

You let it come like a true musician or composer better said.

MR. ALBEE

I know when something is moving, but I'm not going to go around being an audience.

INTERVIEWER

There is something about an emotional detachment in your writing that makes a great play in a way. Do you see what I'm saying?

MR. ALBEE

Well, you shouldn't get in the way of your work.

INTERVIEWER

Right, and sometimes playwrights will. *Their* emotional involvement will come spewing out on the stage.

MR. ALBEE

And then it's no longer the characters, it's the playwright.

INTERVIEWER

Right, right.

MR. ALBEE

That's why I don't write about me. I write through me, not about me. I can't imagine what I can't imagine, so I'm limited by the limits of my imagination. But I don't write about me. I do not exist in any of my plays except as a silent character in *Three Tall Women* perhaps.

INTERVIEWER

Are you overwhelmed at all, sometimes?

MR. ALBEE

About what?

INTERVIEWER

About this thing that happens when a character appears and it's such perfection. It's such a perfection that…

MR. ALBEE

It's very stimulating to know that your mind is working interestingly.

INTERVIEWER

Right. It gets you hot and bothered a little bit.

MR. ALBEE

That's nice. Whoooo, aren't you clever, but then *you* go back to your business. *(He smiles)*

(They both stop for a moment and take each other in. Silence.)

INTERVIEWER

Yeah. *(Looking)* You *are* a Cheshire Cat in a way, you know, with a big wide grin that is… attentive, watching. *(Smiles, shifts again)* Do you get a lot of inspiration at the ocean?

MR. ALBEE

I don't know what inspiration is. I enjoy being by the ocean. I enjoy that a lot. Probably led to *Seascape*.

INTERVIEWER *(Adding)*

Finding the Sun.

MR. ALBEE

Well, *Sandbox* is set on the ocean.

INTERVIEWER

You like bringing the ocean onto stage?

MR. ALBEE

Well, it's very difficult. It's very wet.

INTERVIEWER

It is. It ruins the costumes.

MR. ALBEE

It slops all over into the first row of the orchestra. You can't do that sort of thing.

INTERVIEWER

But the *feeling* of being at the ocean…

MR. ALBEE

I've never counted how many of my plays are outdoors. Quite a few are.

INTERVIEWER

Because you get outdoors, yeah?

MR. ALBEE

Well, my characters do.

INTERVIEWER

Exactly, but in your experience of life it's important to go out, to travel.

MR. ALBEE

Well, contrast is important.

INTERVIEWER

Fine. True enough. *All* contrast is important. Humm, indeed, you never have light without the dark in your plays. They're always quite balanced.

MR. ALBEE

Thank you.

INTERVIEWER

You're welcome. You're welcome. There's constantly a delicate balance that you hold.

MR. ALBEE

Or else it would be *All Over*.

INTERVIEWER

(Knee slap) That's a good one. Indeed. *(Pause)* To what end…

MR. ALBEE

I probably have more four-footed animals in my plays than most people do.

INTERVIEWER

Probably, I think you do.

MR. ALBEE

The dog in the *Zoo Story,* the cat in *Delicate Balance,* the two sea creatures from *Seascape,* the goat in *The Goat.*

INTERVIEWER

But you don't have any animals, do you? I don't see any cats running around.

MR. ALBEE

There is a very old cat upstairs. I used to have Irish Wolfhounds too. They all died. I got too peripatetic to take care of all that.

INTERVIEWER

But now you have a nice old cat.

MR. ALBEE

She's fine.

INTERVIEWER

What's her name?

MR. ALBEE

Snow, she's white, and she's crazy so I called her Snowflake.

INTERVIEWER *(Laughs)*

That's good. It's good to have something moving around the space.

MR. ALBEE

It is.

INTERVIEWER

If not music, then a cat.

MR. ALBEE

I meet lots of dogs on the street, so I get to talk to them.

INTERVIEWER

You like dogs?

MR. ALBEE

Yeah, sure.

INTERVIEWER

Yeah, me too. Irish Wolfhounds? *(Too casual)* What's up with them?

MR. ALBEE *(Not amused)*

"What's up" with them? They're a proper size.

INTERVIEWER

What size are they?

MR. ALBEE

Well, if they stand up and put their paws on your shoulders, they're looking *down* on you.

INTERVIEWER

Wow, wow. *(Laughs)* As do some animals.

175

MR. ALBEE

They're great. I'll have another one someday.

INTERVIEWER

Yeah? They're quiet. They don't talk.

MR. ALBEE

Oh they talk, they don't *jabber*. When they have something to say, they're perfectly happy to talk. They sigh a lot.

INTERVIEWER

(Thinking out loud) When you go to black out, there is never an answer. You never…

MR. ALBEE

Blackout?

INTERVIEWER

In your plays.

MR. ALBEE

Medium fade.

INTERVIEWER

Medium fade. *(Second thought)* Yeah, what is blackout?

MR. ALBEE

(Considering it) I don't know when I do blackouts.

INTERVIEWER

Yeah, I don't know either. You don't. I love… is it in *Tiny Alice*? The stage direction reads: "Not until the lights have gone *completely* down does the curtain drop." Let them sit in the darkness for that moment.

MR. ALBEE

I don't know if I've ever done a blackout. Maybe I have.

INTERVIEWER

Certainly not inside your plays. Maybe scene breaks?

MR. ALBEE

No, they're not blackouts. It's such an artificial device.

INTERVIEWER

It's not real to the world of the play.

MR. ALBEE

No. *(Beat)* It also makes me think that something has happened to the electricity in the theatre.

INTERVIEWER

Indeed. Indeed. The sun rising at the end of *Who's Afraid of Virginia Woolf?* is extraordinary. We've gone through this dark, long night.

MR. ALBEE

"It will be dawn soon I think the party's over. Time to go now."

INTERVIEWER

Yeah. We're done. You know? *(One last thought)* What was the line that you quoted, the funny line… I want to remember.

MR. ALBEE

"After a while, you don't get any drunker, do you?" It's not a question. It's a statement.

177

INTERVIEWER

Thank you. Do you have most of your plays… you know the music by heart?

MR. ALBEE

I can tell when they're being misquoted. Oh sure.

INTERVIEWER

But when you're watching your plays, I know you can hear a misquote very easily I'm sure…

MR. ALBEE

Yeah, but when somebody says I like this line in this play of yours, and they're quoting, I can tell when they're quoting accurately or not.

INTERVIEWER

Right, and they have to quote it accurately because that's the way it's written.

MR. ALBEE

Well, you'd like it that way, but half the time they don't. I mean, I'm talking about interviewers and such. They say, oh that wonderful line and then they misquote it. I have to remind them…

INTERVIEWER

Do you have any wonderful lines that you thought that in a sentence you captured something bigger? "And so it goes." I think of it in *Three Tall Women* where you repeat, I know at least twice, I don't know if I found a third, but I feel like there's a third that I didn't find.

MR. ALBEE

There may be, I'm not sure. No, *she* got fascinated with a phrase, so she repeated it.

INTERVIEWER

I got it. But it's music.

MR. ALBEE

Yeah, it's all music.

INTERVIEWER

And you're always listening to people.

MR. ALBEE

Uh huh.

INTERVIEWER

Not only in your characters, but in life. I know you're a very good listener.

MR. ALBEE

Yeah.

INTERVIEWER

If there is any good secret to playwrighting that could be …

MR. ALBEE

I think listening *helps. (Pause)* I find also that I learn more by listening then I do by talking. *(MR. ALBEE shoots the INTERVIEWER a look.)*

INTERVIEWER *(Packing up his things)*

I like that about your plays, I like that you've said that, that uh, you don't necessarily have the cathartic experience while you watch the play.

MR. ALBEE

After.

INTERVIEWER

After, you prefer.

MR. ALBEE

Yeah. Catharsis after the fact.

INTERVIEWER

Why?

MR. ALBEE

Because otherwise you're just wrapping things up too neatly with too many Christmas ribbons.

INTERVIEWER

Your plays are puzzles to be continually… you know, not *solved*…

MR. ALBEE

Any play you can *get* by seeing it once isn't worth bothering with.

INTERVIEWER

Indeed.

MR. ALBEE

(Long pause) We have to be done.

INTERVIEWER

(Standing up with his things) Thank you Mr. Albee. It's been a real pleasure.

MR. ALBEE

(Quietly) You've done good.

INTERVIEWER

Thanks so much.

(They share a clumsy hug then kiss each other on the cheek. The INTERVIEWER exits slowly. MR. ALBEE is left alone on stage. Silence; tableau. Medium fade to black.)

CURTAIN

Mr. Edward Albee in his Tribeca home, 2005.

ABOUT THE AUTHOR

Eric "Wally" Wallach, has directed, choreographed, produced, and performed in new musicals and original happenings since 1995, primarily in New York City. Shows include: *The Jack of Tarts: a bittersweet musical* (La Mama E.T.C. 2007), *The Breasts of Tiresias: A Surrealist Musical* (Paris, 2010) and *Radical Jew, 33*, his public crucifixion protesting the Iraq War (2005). Wally was also the television host of Manhattan Neighborhood Network's political game show called *Do You Know Anything?!* Wally is also known as Captain Wally Bruce, the creator of *FLIGHT18*, offering space travel for all since 2010. The propellent of the Spaceship Kaleidoscope is the spontaneous combustion of humans dancing and playing in the stars. Wally is also a co-director of Brooklyn Arts for Kids and a popular teaching artist with Theatre Development Fund. He brings his own approach to theatre collaboration to students of all ages throughout New York City and beyond. Wally has a BA in Theatre from San Diego State University, where he honed his multi-arts exploration of theatre. Wally is a torchbearer of the artists he has had the honor of working with, including Jack O'Brien, Robert Wilson, Joseph Chaikin, and Penny Arcade. His writing is found in periodicals such as the Bridge Journal and The Brooklyn Rail, along with this book and the forthcoming *Make Theatre Now*. He is a longtime member of SAG/AFTRA and founding member of the Lower East Side Biography Project. Finally, he is a Los Angeles-born hippie, Girl Dad, and BikeDancer. For more scripts, articles, photos, and videos, browse around www.ebwally.com.

PEACE

and links for all.

Made in the USA
Columbia, SC
09 February 2025